JOHN PROCTOR IS THE VILLAIN

A PLAY BY KIMBERLY BELFLOWER

JOHN PROCTOR IS THE VILLAIN
Copyright © 2024, Kimberly Belflower

All Rights Reserved

JOHN PROCTOR IS THE VILLAIN is fully protected under the copyright laws of the United States of America, and of all countries covered by the International Copyright Union (including the Dominion of Canada and the rest of the British Commonwealth), and of all countries covered by the Pan-American Copyright Convention, the Universal Copyright Convention, the Berne Convention, and of all countries with which the United States has reciprocal copyright relations. No part of this publication may be reproduced in any form by any means (electronic, mechanical, photocopying, recording, or otherwise), or stored in any retrieval system in any way (electronic or mechanical) without written permission of the publisher.

The English language stock stage performance rights in the United States, its territories, possessions and Canada and the amateur stage performance rights throughout the world for JOHN PROCTOR IS THE VILLAIN are controlled exclusively by Broadway Licensing, www.BroadwayLicensing.com. **No professional or nonprofessional performance of the Play may be given without obtaining in advance the written permission of Broadway Licensing and paying the requisite fee.**

All other rights, including without limitation motion picture, recitation, lecturing, public reading, radio broadcasting, television, video or sound recording, and the rights of translation into foreign languages are strictly reserved.

Inquiries concerning all other rights should be addressed to WME Entertainment, 11 Madison Avenue, New York, NY 10010. Attn: Michael Finkle.

NOTE ON BILLING

Anyone receiving permission to produce JOHN PROCTOR IS THE VILLAIN is required to give credit to the Author as sole and exclusive Author of the Play on the title page of all programs distributed in connection with performances of the Play and in all instances in which the title of the Play appears, including printed or digital materials for advertising, publicizing or otherwise exploiting the Play and/or a production thereof. Please see your production license for font size and typeface requirements.

Be advised that there may be additional credits required in all programs and promotional material. Such language will be listed under the "Additional Billing" section of production licenses. It is the licensee's responsibility to ensure any and all required billing is included in the requisite places, per the terms of the license.

SPECIAL NOTE ON SONGS/RECORDINGS

"Green Light," written by Jack Antonoff, Joel Little, and Ella Yelich-O'Connor, is required for performance. The rights to the song are included with the written performance license for the Play. Please see your license for materials and additional billing information.

Broadway Licensing neither holds the rights to nor grants permission to use any songs or recordings mentioned in the Play. Permission for performances of copyrighted songs, arrangements or recordings mentioned in this Play is not included in our license agreement. The permission of the copyright owner(s) must be obtained for any such use. For any songs and/or recordings mentioned in the Play, other songs, arrangements, or recordings may be substituted provided permission from the copyright owner(s) of such songs, arrangements or recordings is obtained; or songs, arrangements or recordings in the public domain may be substituted.

SPECIAL NOTE ON THE CRUCIBLE

Neither the title *The Crucible* nor any portion of *The Crucible*, nor Arthur Miller's name in the title, any subtitle, or any "log line" may be used in connection with any advertising or promotion of the Play or any production of the Play, and neither Arthur Miller's likeness or biography may be used in connection with any advertising or promotion of the Play or any production of the Play.

A NOTE ON EXCERPTS

Selections from *The Crucible* by Arthur Miller are included in the script for JOHN PROCTOR IS THE VILLAIN with express permission of the Arthur Miller 2004 Literary and Dramatic Property Trust.

JOHN PROCTOR IS THE VILLAIN premiered on Broadway at the Booth Theatre in March 2025, produced by Sue Wagner, John Johnson, John Mara, Jr., Runyonland, Eric Falkenstein, and Jillian Robbins. It was directed by Danya Taymor; the associate director was Autumn Angelettie; the dramaturg was Lauren Halvorsen; the scenography was by AMP ft. Teresa L. Williams; the costume design was by Sarah Laux; the lighting design was by Natasha Katz; the sound design and original composition were by Palmer Hefferan; the projection design was by Hannah Wasileski; the hair and makeup design was by J. Jared Janas; the movement was by Tilly Evans-Krueger; the casting was by Taylor Williams; the intimacy direction was by Ann James; the vocal, text, and dialect coach was Gigi Buffington; and the production stage manager was Kamra A. Jacobs. The cast was as follows:

CARTER SMITH	Gabriel Ebert
SHELBY HOLCOMB	Sadie Sink
BETH POWELL	Fina Strazza
NELL SHAW	Morgan Scott
IVY WATKINS	Maggie Kuntz
RAELYNN NIX	Amalia Yoo
MASON ADAMS	Nihar Duvvuri
LEE TURNER	Hagan Oliveras
BAILEY GALLAGHER	Molly Griggs
UNDERSTUDIES	Noah Pacht, Fiona Robberson, Shian Tomlinson, Victoria Vourkoutiotis, and Garrett Young

JOHN PROCTOR IS THE VILLAIN was originally produced by Studio Theatre (David Muse, Artistic Director; Rebecca Ende Lichtenberg, Managing Director), Washington, DC, in May 2022. It was directed by Marti Lyons, the assistant director was Francesca Sabel, the dramaturg was Adrien-Alice Hansel, the set design was by Luciana Stecconi, the costume design was by Moyenda Kulemeka, the lighting design was by Jesse Belsky, the sound design and composition was by Kathy Ruvuna, the props design was by Deb Thomas, the fight coach was Chelsea Pace, the dialect and vocal coach was Nancy Krebs, the casting was by the Telsey Office, the assistant stage manager was Stephen Bubniak, and the production stage manager was Madison Bahr. The cast was as follows:

CARTER SMITH .... Dave Register
SHELBY HOLCOMB .... Juliana Sass
BETH POWELL .... Miranda Rizzolo
NELL SHAW .... Deidre Staples
IVY WATKINS .... Resa Mishina
RAELYNN NIX .... Jordan Slattery
MASON ADAMS .... Ignacio Diaz-Silverio,
                                         Shawn Denegre-Vaught
LEE TURNER .... Zachary Keller
BAILEY GALLAGHER .... Lida Maria Benson
UNDERSTUDIES .... Mollie Greenburg, Lauren Fraites,
                    J. Bradley Bowers, Bowen Fox, Martha Epstein,
                          Tre'Mon Kentrell Mills, and Julia Souza

JOHN PROCTOR IS THE VILLAIN was produced at Huntington Theatre Company (Loretta Greco, Norma Jean Calderwood Artistic Director; Christopher Mannelli, Executive Director), Boston, Massachusetts, in February 2024. It was directed by Margot Bordelon, the assistant director was Carla Mirabal Rodríguez, the dramaturg was Lauren Halvorsen, the choreography was by Victoria Lynn Awkward, the scenic design was by Kristen Robinson, the cosume design was by Zoë Sundra, the lighting design was by Aja M. Jackson, the sound design was by Sinan Refik Zafar, the hair and wig design was by Rachel Padula-Shufelt, the fight and intimacy consultant was Jessica Scout Malone, the voice and dialect coach was Christine Hamel, the casting was by Dale Brown, the production stage manager was Emily F. McMullen, the line producer was Kevin Schlagle, the production assistants were Kendyll Trot and Winnie Chang, and the stage managers were Lucas Bryce Dixon and Ashley Pitchford. The cast was as follows:

CARTER SMITH .... Japhet Balaban
SHELBY HOLCOMB .... Isabel Van Natta
BETH POWELL .... Jules Talbot
NELL SHAW .... Victoria Omoregie
IVY WATKINS .... Brianna Martinez
RAELYNN NIX .... Haley Wong
MASON ADAMS .... Maanav Aryan Goyal
LEE TURNER .... Benjamin Izaak
BAILEY GALLAGHER .... Olivia Hebert
UNDERSTUDIES .... Jaime Jose Hernandez,
        Patrick O'Konis, Valyn Lyric Turner, Jack Greenberg,
        Katherine Callaway, Zehava Younger, and Jessica Golden

JOHN PROCTOR IS THE VILLAIN was commissioned by the Farm Theater's College Collaboration Project (Padraic Lillis, Artistic Director) and developed with Centre College, Rollins College, and Furman University.

JOHN PROCTOR IS THE VILLAIN was developed at Ojai Playwrights Conference (Robert Egan, Artistic Director/Producer).

acknowledgments

Hannah Wolf, Casey Stangl, Sasha Emerson, Tiffany Moon, and Lauren Halvorsen: heroes + early champions of JP and me, who have all had a hand in changing my life.

Padraic Lillis, and the 2018-19 students and theatre faculty of Centre College, Rollins College, and Furman University: you are in every page.

I met my partner, Dan Stemmerman, when theatre shut down in 2020. his love, curiosity, and full-throttle support of this play and my work during an incredibly dark time helped me hold onto hope.

my mama, Suzanne Belflower; my dad, Buddy Belflower; my brother, Jeff Belflower; my sister-in-law, Katie Powell Belflower; my nephew/favorite person, Henry Belflower. thank you for going to see iterations of this play at colleges and cities across the country, for giving me my love of the mountains and the rural South, and for always giving me a soft place to land.

Marti Lyons, Adrien-Alice Hansel, Margot Bordelon, Lauren Halvorsen (again): your wisdom, artistry, rigor, and friendship are forever essential pillars keeping this play upright.
Juliana Sass, Francesca Sabel: long live.
Michael Finkle: for getting it and never giving up.
Kevin Poole: for ghostwriting arguably the best line in the play.
Alison and the Etheridge family: for helping me become me.
Blake Daniel: my bones.
Devin Horne: for so graciously loaning me a story.
my students at Emory University: for teaching me so much.

all my friends and teachers, but especially for this play: Cortney Knipp, Megan Tabaque, Drew Paryzer, Collin Stapleton, Liz Engelman, Steven Dietz, Kirk Lynn, Sam Provenzano, Victoria Rey, Mallory Nonnemaker, Krystine Summers, Maia Macdonald, Amber Hughes, Krista Maggart, Caroline Thrasher, Caitlin Hargraves, Taylor Trensch, Jared Loftin, Barrett Weed, Jenn Damiano, Kathryn de la Rosa.

Gail Jones: always. this play and my life wouldn't exist without you.

characters*

CARTER SMITH, teacher, mid to late 30s, M. a former golden boy, but one of those rare smart and sensitive ones. now he's a great teacher: charming, engaging, goofy.

SHELBY HOLCOMB, student, 16, F. her brain works faster than her mouth, but her mouth works pretty dang fast. people have always underestimated her.

BETH POWELL, student, 17, F. nervous and ambitious and enthusiastic. kind of like if Rory Gilmore and Paris Geller had a baby and raised her in the Deep South.

NELL SHAW, student, 16, F. from Atlanta. grounded and sincere. genuinely curious about things. a good judge of character, and a quick study.

IVY WATKINS, student, 17, F. fiercely loyal and always well-intentioned. from money. resist the urge to play her as a mean girl.

RAELYNN NIX, student, 16, F. a cheerleader type who's always lived her life by other people's standards. she was paying careful attention and keeping score the whole time.

MASON ADAMS, student, 17, M. he's never really tried before, and he's surprised by how good it feels. earnest and affable.

LEE TURNER, student, 16, M. a carhartt-wearing good ol' boy. deeply insecure and without the tools to deal with it. he's always been good at getting what he wants.

BAILEY GALLAGHER, counselor, 24, F. sweet in all the ways Southern women are supposed to be. this is her first real job out of college. she's trying her best.

---

* you can have as many other students present for the classroom scenes as you have room and resources for

time and place

spring semester, junior year, 2018
Helen County High, the only high school in a one-stoplight town, northeast Georgia
all scenes are in Mr. Smith's classroom unless noted

a note on casting

rural Georgia doesn't mean all white. never has.
the case can be made for any of these girls (and Mason) to be a person of color, but certain combinations lead to stereotypes and/or commentary I'm not trying to make. as such:
- Nell is Black, but if at all possible, she shouldn't be the only POC onstage.
- Nell and Shelby shouldn't be the only POC.
- Lee and Mr. Smith are white. full stop. I imagine Beth is white too, given the nature of her fumbles and oversights, but she can also be a non-Black POC.

a note on dialect

I'd rather have no dialect than a bad one. but if you go for it—Appalachian Southern is quite different than standard Southern. some characters probably have thicker accents than others, depending on their family and upbringing.

a note on dialogue, pace, and quiet

the page count might be high, but this play moves very, very quickly. if it's over 1:45ish you're going too slow. NO INTERMISSION!!!
a beat is a breath. but like, a *full* breath—inhale, exhale. a pause is 2–3 beats. a long pause is longer than that. a moment is even longer.
use line breaks, capitalization, and punctuation as clues for importance, pace, and shifts in thought. a slash ("/") indicates an overlap in speech. whenever a "/" appears, the next line of dialogue should immediately begin.

"I am trusting
well-adjusted
marked me dormant
I erupted."

—Charly Bliss, "Chatroom"

"We have to be the witches they've always said we are, and counter their magic with our own. So fine, if you insist. This is a witch hunt. We're witches, and we're hunting you."
—Lindy West, *The Witches Are Coming*

"The New England woman had no political rights. She neither voted nor served on juries. Officially voiceless, she nonetheless found plenty of ways to make herself heard and demonstrated a vaulting need to speak her mind. In legal records she hectors, shrieks, quarrels, scolds, rants, rails, tattles, and spits."
—Stacy Schiff, *The Witches: Salem, 1692*

JOHN PROCTOR IS THE VILLAIN

1.

a high school classroom
everyone has the same textbook open to the same spot

MR. SMITH.
"sex"

THE ENTIRE CLASS.
(in unison)
"the biologic character or quality that distinguishes male and female from one another as expressed by analysis of the person's gonadal, morphologic, chromosomal, and hormonal characteristics."

MR. SMITH.
or…

THE ENTIRE CLASS.
(in unison)
"the physiologic and psychological processes within a person that prompt behavior related to procreation or erotic pleasure."

MR. SMITH.
Lee…
that's enough
any questions so far?

    beat

I know it seems really lame, guys
believe me
I remember being exactly where you are

and feeling like "are you kidding me?"
but this is the curriculum
these are the facts

IVY.
but I mean doesn't it make sense for sex ed to actually come like before people know about sex?

NELL.
yeah like
I had sex ed in fifth grade when I still lived in Atlanta

a scandalized beat

MR. SMITH.
that's a good point, Ivy
and Nell's right—
many schools, especially in bigger cities,
believe in teaching these things much earlier
and I guess it just comes down to philosophy
I guess here
we believe you're not ready for big ideas like this when you're younger

Beth suddenly raises her hand

MR. SMITH.
yes! Beth!

BETH.
sorry!
for interrupting

MR. SMITH.
not at all
go for it

BETH.
okay
sorry
but like

I mean
why do you have to be the one to teach us about se—
this material
in the first place?
it just feels like we've wasted so much lit time
which is
I mean the syllabus is so good
I'm worried we won't have enough time to dig deep into the reading

MASON.
dude
why are you freaking out
about doing less work

MR. SMITH.
well, you know
we're almost finished
it's only a six week unit, ten minutes per class
not too bad in the scheme of things

BETH.
no of course
I'm sorry
I didn't mean to sound like I was complaining

MR. SMITH.
no no no
I didn't mean to sound like I was minimizing the way you feel
and honestly?
it has been kind of a bummer
that time adds up
and look
let's be real
I know you guys already know about sex…
but you know
I'm gonna level with you
there have been some uh
unfortunate cuts in the last few years
and we're all just pitching in as best we can

at the end of the day, it's now part of my job to make sure you hear this info
so let's just muscle through it together, yeah?
then we'll get to some stuff I actually like teaching
and that you actually like learning
at least I hope so

> *some laughter from the class*

this next stretch of the semester is my favorite
we've got *The Crucible* up next, for the rest of the month!
we've got *Wuthering Heights* later on
very spooky, very romantic

> *Beth raises her hand again*

BETH.
also!
sorry!
just wondering
I mean speaking of *The Crucible*
I know on the syllabus it said the drama unit starts today
is that still true?

NELL.
do you have the syllabus memorized?

IVY.
she Absolutely does

> *some giggles*

NELL.
but honestly yeah same
like
are we gonna talk about this play or what

MR. SMITH.
if we can make it through the rest of these definitions
we'll start the drama unit today as planned

> *some slight panic*

a lot of people forgot to do the reading for the drama unit

I don't know what all these panicked looks are about
since I'm sure everyone already did the reading for today

BETH.
yes!

MR. SMITH.
anyone besides Beth?
act one of *The Crucible*?
right?

some other vague murmurs

okay look
this is a really important play
and it's on me for not reminding you about the reading
so
how about I give you until later this week to finish act one

a few small cheers

okay great we like that idea
and then today how about I just tell you why this play is so awesome
that way we can all be on the same page for our first discussion
sound good?

general murmurs of agreement
Mason raises his hand

MASON.
so we're reading like
the Whole Play?

MR. SMITH.
yes we are
the whole play
but come on, you guys!
we're gonna have a lot of fun
read some scenes out loud together…
were any of you in drama before it got cut?

Beth and Ivy raise their hands

nice
and! *The Crucible* is gonna be the basis for that infamous junior lit interpretive project
you'll get your partners next week

> *a couple of groans*
> *Beth sits up straighter*

anyway
so
The Crucible
lately we've heard the term "witch hunt" a lot
people love to use that phrase, right?
its usage has definitely become more casual over time,
but basically it's referring to this really dark period in history
that here in America, reached its peak during the Salem Witch Trials in 1692
over *two hundred people* in Salem, Massachusetts, were accused of practicing witchcraft
and *twenty* of those people were executed
but later we found out that all those accusations were untrue
innocent people died
and why?
largely: mass hysteria, spurred on by various things we'll get into later
so when people say "witch hunt"
they're basically saying "a bunch of people are saying untrue things that could become dangerous if left unchecked"
so
cut to: the 1950s
Arthur Miller, the guy who wrote *The Crucible*, was living through another time of widespread panic:
Senator Joseph McCarthy had terrified the entire country into thinking that
communism had infiltrated the American government
he started having all these hearings with people he suspected
and even though a lot of people disagreed with him

they weren't really willing to cross him
they were afraid of being seen as disloyal or being accused themselves
so we saw this moment in time when a lot of innocent people got taken down
because a lot of other people got carried away
just like in Salem
so Arthur Miller wrote *The Crucible* as an allegory for McCarthyism
do we remember what an "allegory" / is?

> *Nell and Beth's hands fly up at the same time and they both start speaking before Mr. Smith finishes*

NELL.
a symbolic work / where characters and events represent other ideas

BETH.
a symbolic work in which the characters and events represent other ideas, often political in nature

NELL.
(friendly competition)
beat you!

> *Beth has never been bested in school before
> it's a little horrible and a little exhilarating*

MR. SMITH.
yes!
awesome! both of you!
he was like "hey guys we've been here before, and it didn't go too well"
we continue to repeat our history if we don't learn from it, right?
unless we speak truth in times of untruth
and the person in *The Crucible* who does this is John Proctor
one of the best characters ever
he had an affair with Abigail Williams, one of the other main characters, a while back—
no spoilers, you find out almost right away—
and Abigail is like really determined to get revenge

she becomes kind of a ringleader to everyone making these accusations
and it gets pre-tty crazy
anyway
I'm really excited to dig into this with y'all
I think it's a gift that we get to study material like this
I mean obviously what's going on out there in the world
and right here, where we live…
it's a really intense time
but that's what literature is for
that's what art is for
to make sense of moments in time like this one

Beth might clutch her heart

any questions?
awesome
okay
so let's power through these last definitions, yeah?
I bet if we really go for it, we can finish the rest of the unit today…
right where we left off
most important one
everybody ready?

he waits until everybody's ready

"abstinence"

THE ENTIRE CLASS.
(in unison)
"the act or practice of choosing to refrain from having sex and the only method one hundred percent guaranteed to prevent pregnancy or disease."

MR. SMITH.
awesome

2.

> *later the same day*
> *after school, 4 PM*
> *Beth, Nell, Ivy, and Raelynn meet with the school counselor,*
> *Miss Gallagher*
> *mid argument*

MISS GALLAGHER.
it's just that some people feel like this will alienate the boys

BETH.
but boys can be members

IVY.
they *should* be members

NELL.
also who even feels that way?

MISS GALLAGHER.
I'm not
at liberty to say

BETH.
but maybe if we were able to foster a meaningful dialogue with them
we could find common ground
that's like
the whole purpose of this club
that's why it's so important

MISS GALLAGHER.
it's just
a tricky situation
with everything that's been going on in the community…
people are—
tensions
are high
you have to understand that

IVY.
our tensions are high too!
we need an outlet!

NELL.
yeah I don't understand why tension in the community means we have to suffer

MISS GALLAGHER.
okay now
let's choose our words with care
y'all are hardly *suffering*

NELL.
yeah but
suffering is subjective, so

MISS GALLAGHER.
I'm going to have to ask you *all* to check your tone

NELL.
oh my god??

MISS GALLAGHER.
look
I know they must have done things different in Atlanta—
and I really wish I could help you /
I do, but

IVY.
I think they "do things different" everywhere now
it's 2018

BETH.
helping us is literally within your power as our counselor

MISS GALLAGHER.
I think you're overestimating the amount of power I have here

NELL.
you should be fighting for us

MISS GALLAGHER.
I am

BETH.
how?

MISS GALLAGHER.
listen
this is a small town

BETH.
that doesn't answer my question like at all

MISS GALLAGHER.
we have to be aware of the effect our actions can have on / the—

> *Mr. Smith enters the classroom, just as Beth loses it*

BETH.
yeah we DO have to be aware of that
and I mean like it is literally your job to facilitate situations like this!!!
just do your job!!!!

MR. SMITH.
whoa whoa whoa—
what's going on in here?

> *Beth claps a hand over her mouth, horrified at herself*
> *beat*

MISS GALLAGHER.
these girls came to me to see why their club proposal got rejected
and I have been trying to explain to them
that it's a sensitive issue
with many complicated
things
and I empathize with them
I do
but they are not showing me the respect / I

BETH.
Miss Gallagher I'm so so sorry
I didn't mean to snap at you like that I—
I'm so so sorry
I'm just really passionate about this
and I got / upset

MR. SMITH.
I'm sure Miss Gallagher here knows what a good student you are, Beth
what a great girl
and I'm sure she knows it won't happen again

BETH.
it won't
it absolutely won't

MISS GALLAGHER.
it's
all right

MR. SMITH.
could someone else fill me in on what's happening here?
what's this club?

>   *beat*

NELL.
it's a feminism club

RAELYNN.
yeah it's supposed to like—
Beth what's the way you said it?

BETH.
spread awareness, foster dialogue, and ignite change

MR. SMITH.
what a great idea
and a very well-worded mission, Beth, awesome work

>   *Beth totally blooms*

BETH.
thank you

IVY.
Nell had one at her school in Atlanta

MISS GALLAGHER.
which is great
but I was just explaining to the girls why
even though I am totally and completely on their side
feminism is just
people are sensitive right now
and maybe the girls can have these conversations on their own for the time being
then later
when the time is right
we can bring / it into the

BETH.
but we need to start it before senior year
or it won't look like a long-term commitment for college
plus it's literally perfect for right now!
I mean Me Too stuff is like
all over the news

MR. SMITH.
I wonder if there's another solution here
I'm just spitballing
but what if we frame it more like a lit thing?
get some other students involved, maybe some boys…
sneak the feminism in kind of under the radar
maybe we could find some reading to tie it all into our work with *The Crucible*
I could even be the faculty sponsor if you think that might help

the girls are thrilled

BETH.
that's an AMAZING idea

MISS GALLAGHER.
well hold on we don't want to get ahead of ourselves
but the curriculum tie is an interesting—
and it is possible that having a male sponsor would probably help some of / the

MR. SMITH.
I'd be happy to take on any pushback
help the girls shape what they do here
make sure no feathers get ruffled
that don't need to get ruffled

MISS GALLAGHER.
I think there might be a few things to discuss with Principal / David

MR. SMITH.
oh of course of course
you just tell me what we should do next
can I put my name on any forms?

MISS GALLAGHER.
why don't we go see if he's in his office
girls, you hold tight

BETH.
thank you Miss Gallagher!!

> *Miss Gallagher leaves*
> *Mr. Smith prepares to follow*
> *he stops at the door, turns back, and winks*
> *he leaves*

IVY.
yay!!!

NELL.
he is so amazing
he's like
the teacher in an inspirational movie

BETH.
I thought you were mad at him because of sex ed

NELL.
I was never *mad*
and especially not at *him*
I was frustrated with the *system*
public schools are broken

IVY.
he's
So Hot

BETH.
(rolling her eyes)
oh my lord
here we go

RAELYNN.
I know you think so too

BETH.
I don't think about him like that
I told you

IVY.
liar

BETH.
I *don't!!*

NELL.
well I most certainly do

IVY.
his *shoulders* are just

NELL.
were you watching when he dropped the chalk* last week?
when he bent over to get it?

---

* or "eraser"

IVY.
oh my god wait have you seen how big his feet are?

NELL.
big feet don't necessarily mean anything about like
the size of other things

IVY.
yeah but
he wore these sweatpants to relay for life last year and like…

laughter

BETH.
you guys stop!
he's like
my friend

IVY.
oh Beth

BETH.
I know it sounds weird but he is!
my mom says I'm an old soul!

IVY.
(to Nell)
thank god you're here now
little miss old soul never talks about sweatpants dick with me

BETH.
IVY!!

IVY.
(to Nell, re Raelynn)
neither does little miss preacher's daughter

RAELYNN.
he's not my type
(to Nell)
it's really cool though, all the honors lit classes go to his house for
dinner at the end of the year

NELL.
shut up
I bet his house is like
impeccably decorated

RAELYNN.
and his wife doesn't even do most of the cooking
he does

IVY.
he's like
the only adult I know who doesn't treat us like elementary schoolers

BETH.
yeah he really respects us

NELL.
not like Miss Gallagher
"I know they must do things different in Atlanta"
that was some bullshit

IVY.
it's SO WEIRD to think she's only like
eight years older than us

NELL.
wait
really?

BETH.
I think that's a big part of it
she's like trying to be a Real Adult

IVY.
yeah my sister's twenty and Miss Gallagher was a senior when she was a freshman

RAELYNN.
she was a cheerleader
me and Ivy used to go to cheer camp when we were little and like learn dances from her

IVY.
then she went to college for counseling or whatever
and Ms. Cole was retiring when she graduated so now she's back here

BETH.
I can't believe I yelled at her

RAELYNN.
it's fine
you're fine

BETH.
I just
do you think any of this will mess with college?
like is she gonna write down in my file that I was disrespectful?

IVY.
oh my god that's not a thing

NELL.
it could actually like *help* with college
everywhere worth going would love that you spoke truth to power

IVY.
also why are you so worried about college all the time
the lowest grade you've ever gotten was like a ninety-six

BETH.
grades here are different though
we live in a one-stoplight town in Georgia

IVY.
oh!
my dad says we're getting another stoplight!

BETH.
it doesn't matter!!
when colleges look at my application they're either gonna feel sorry
for me
or think I'm like
a horse

IVY.
Beth what

RAELYNN.
I love horses

IVY.
well yeah they're perfect
remember I did horse therapy that one summer

NELL.
oh so you're like *rich*

IVY.
I love that that's your takeaway
not like, "oh dang what did you need horse therapy for, are you okay?"

NELL.
I mean
does anybody *need* horse therapy?

IVY.
yeah!
they do!
it's really beneficial and it helped me a lot!!!

Beth puts her arm around Ivy

BETH.
Ivy wants to be a large-animal vet

NELL.
okay Beth
let's get down to business
feminism club
what's first on the agenda

BETH.
I mean
I don't want to get ahead of ourselves
what if we still don't get approved?

NELL.
fuck that
we'll like
go to buzzfeed or something
make this ish go viral
(very buzzfeed voice)
"forbidden feminism in Appalachia—1900s or now?"

IVY.
"the answer might surprise you!"

BETH.
I guess we *could* start planning, just for fun…
I have a lot of ideas already, but I would love to hear your suggestions

RAELYNN.
I think we should read *Twilight*

BETH.
no

IVY.
Raelynn, why are you so obsessed with *Twilight*?
it came out when we were like seven

BETH.
there are so many other books

RAELYNN.
yeah but you know my dad won't let me read anything he hasn't read first
so he can like make sure it's appropriate
but in *Twilight* they save themselves for marriage so

NELL.
ohhh right isn't there something crazy with vampire sex or whatever

BETH.
it's just not very feminist

RAELYNN.
why not?

NELL.
because Bella's just obsessed with a guy, right?

RAELYNN.
yeah but she does a lot of other stuff too
plus I mean Edward's like a mega-feminist
which is so weird because he's actually from like the gilded age or whatever

BETH.
Victorian

RAELYNN.
but like
we can be obsessed with guys and still be feminists, right?

IVY.
I thought you broke up with him

RAELYNN.
this is not about Lee like at all
this is about *Twilight*

NELL.
I like *The Craft*

RAELYNN.
I don't know what that is

IVY.
is that the old movie about witches?
isn't it like really dark?

NELL.
I like dark stuff
female rage

RAELYNN.
I do love witches

IVY.
since when?

RAELYNN.
um since forever??
remember fifth grade?
I did that project on the Salem Witch Trials and wrote in my diary as one of the girls
like in character or whatever?

IVY.
oh riiiight oh my god I forgot about that

BETH.
wait didn't you name one of your dolls Tituba

RAELYNN.
it's a really pretty name

NELL.
I saw a production of *The Crucible* where a white girl played Tituba so that was a choice

RAELYNN.
but my dad was Not like
happy about doll-Tituba
because of the devil
so I told him I changed her name to Mary
but her real name is still Tituba
it's just a secret now

beat

BETH.
we could talk about Taylor Swift

NELL.
jesus Beth

BETH.
there is a LOT to unpack!
we can fully address her past mistakes and problematic aspects

and how far she's come
by like
talking about intersectional feminism and stuff
also if we're gonna talk about Me Too, her trial was pretty major

NELL.
pass

IVY.
I liked her before her music got all sexual

RAELYNN.
you were just talking about Mr. Smith's feet, you perv

BETH.
and his *sweatpants*

IVY.
I'm not flaunting that to the world through my music!

NELL.
okay so Beth, it sounds like we should add sex positivity to the list of ideas

RAELYNN.
also *Speak Now* came out in 2010 and had lyrics that were very sexually charged
so it's not really a new thing for her

IVY.
what
were the sexual lyrics in *Speak Now*

RAELYNN.
it's like you've never even listened to "Sparks Fly"

NELL.
I do kinda like that song she wrote about john mayer

> *the girls might sing from the bridge of "Dear John"* –*
> *a progression/escalation that Ivy starts*

---

* see note on songs/recordings at the back of this volume

they all love this song, they grew up on it

BETH.
I think about that part all the time
I cannot wait to shine over this sad empty town

RAELYNN.
I kind of hope she murders john mayer one day

BETH.
what??

RAELYNN.
but like
in a very very sneaky way
like no one will know it's her
but I'll know
he'll just turn up dead one day from like "natural causes"
and I'll be like
yeah girl
yes
you did it

    beat

IVY.
so wait
have you or have you not been talking to Lee?

RAELYNN.
I genuinely want Taylor Swift to murder john mayer
and I don't have anything to say to Lee
so no

IVY.
okay

    beat

have you talked to Shelby?

RAELYNN.
who?

BETH.
Raelynn

RAELYNN.
I don't know a Shelby

    beat

NELL.
I also don't know a Shelby?
but from the vibe in here I feel like maybe mine is different…

RAELYNN.
if this is feminism club
why are we talking about something that's like
the opposite of feminism?

IVY.
I was just asking
I'm kind of like worried about her

BETH.
same

RAELYNN.
well I'm not

IVY.
I texted her like ten times before I gave up

BETH.
Nell, Raelynn's boyfriend cheated on her with this girl Shelby—

RAELYNN.
BETH!

BETH.
she's our friend now!
she should know what's going on!

RAELYNN.
we've gotten through this much of the frickin semester without telling her!
why do we have to start now??

BETH.
fine
I'm sorry

NELL.
I won't like
tell anybody

RAELYNN.
I mean everybody already knows
I wasn't like keeping it from you
it was just nice to know that one person wasn't talking about it

    pause

fine
so like
(rapid-fire, she wants to get this over with)
Shelby used to be my best friend in the whole world like since we were little kids but last semester she started acting different and then she like seduced my boyfriend and I'm not just letting him get away with it either don't worry but it sucked a lot I mean obviously and then she stopped coming to school and now she's been gone for like three months or like four I guess since November anyway we don't know where she is or if she's coming back and that's what you missed on *Glee*

3.

> *one week later*
> *morning, before first bell*
> *Lee is alone, sitting at a desk, waiting*
> *Raelynn enters*

LEE.
hey

> *Raelynn immediately turns around to leave*
> *Lee jumps up and blocks her exit*

hey hey hey
no no no
c'mon baby please just listen to me—

RAELYNN.
I'll scream

> *Lee covers her mouth with his hand*
> *they stand there like that for a moment*
> *it's a little charged*
> *Lee takes his hand away and kisses Raelynn, hard*
> *she tries to squirm away*

stop it

> *Lee keeps kissing her*

Lee
I'm serious

> *Lee keeps kissing her*

STOP

> *she smacks him, hard*

LEE.
jesus

RAELYNN.
I told you

LEE.
you were kissing me back

RAELYNN.
for like a second

>*she starts to go out the door again
Lee grabs her hand and yanks her back*

LEE.
Raelynn
please
I just wanna talk to you

>*Lee still has her hand in his*

RAELYNN.
what are you even doing here
you're never early

LEE.
yeah but you are
you used to hang out in the lunchroom
I've been waitin there for like a week

RAELYNN.
Mr. Smith says this is a safe space for whoever needs it
I haven't felt like being around everybody

LEE.
I'm not everybody

RAELYNN.
will you let me have my hand back please

LEE.
I don't want to

>*beat*

RAELYNN.
honestly Lee maybe
I don't know
it might be good that this happened?
you know?
like I think maybe it was supposed to?
like maybe it's actually better this way?

Lee lets go of her hand

LEE.
why
why are you saying that?
why are you acting like this?
I just / don't

RAELYNN.
we've been together for seven years
Lee that's not normal
we're only sixteen
we've been going out since fourth grade
it's so weird

LEE.
I don't think it's weird

RAELYNN.
I like
…
…
I think I'm starting to realize like
I don't really um
I have no idea who I am without you?
I mean
being your girlfriend has been like
the main thing in my life, like it's been everything?
and I just
I'm not sure that's the way it should be

LEE.
that used to be okay
you used to like that

RAELYNN.
I don't know if I did
I think maybe I just didn't think about it

LEE.
you don't have to think about every single thing
you know?
sometimes things can just be whatever they are

RAELYNN.
I like thinking about things
I wanna think about more things
I wanna try more stuff

LEE.
like what
kissing other guys?

RAELYNN.
no!
I mean maybe
one day
but that's not even in like
the top five

LEE.
what is?

RAELYNN.
I don't know!
that's the point!
I don't even know what I wanna try!
I don't know anything!

LEE.
you obviously have Something in mind
or Someone

RAELYNN.
you're not listening to me you never listen to me

LEE.
I am listening, you're just not telling the truth

RAELYNN.
I don't know!
I wanna dress different maybe!

LEE.
right
to get attention from different guys

RAELYNN.
no!
god!
why are You mad at Me for hypothetically wanting to kiss other guys when *you* did way more than kiss with my BEST FRIEND

LEE.
I made a mistake
and jesus
I wanna make up for it
but you're not giving me a chance
I miss you
okay?
I love you
baby, you're my whole world

RAELYNN.
the world is really big
I'm just one person

LEE.
…
this isn't you
all this stuff you're saying
it's like
fuckin Beth

and that new Atlanta girl
and that club

RAELYNN.
we only started the club like
last week
and it's / not like

LEE.
look

>   *beat*

I was frustrated
I mean like
it's different for guys

RAELYNN.
no I get that

LEE.
we'd been together for *seven years*

RAELYNN.
we've covered that yeah

LEE.
like
is it your dad?
I thought all that stuff from church wasn't really
I mean what are you waiting for?

RAELYNN.
I'm not waiting *for* anything
I don't know

LEE.
do you not trust me?

RAELYNN.
I mean
obviously I don't *now*

> *beat*
> *Lee shakes his head to himself*
> *then he pushes over a desk kinda violently*
> *like, he throws it a little*
> *not directly at Raelynn or anything*
> *he doesn't like hulk out or go crazy*
> *it's just a moment of casual violence*
> *it makes you wonder how many times Lee's done stuff like this*
> *it makes you think about all the casual violence you've witnessed and excused*
> *it makes you think about that time in college acting class when a guy punched a hole through the wall right next to his female scene partner and your professor praised him for being "truthful"*
> *it makes you think about how many times you've heard "boys will be boys"*
> *Raelynn jumps back*

Lee!!!

> *beat*

LEE.
sorry

> *beat*

sorry
I just

> *long pause*

RAELYNN.
I'm gonna go like
get breakfast or something
before the bell

> *Raelynn starts to leave*

LEE.
hey
why are you wearing so much stuff on your eyes lately?

    beat

RAELYNN.
I like it
I like the way it looks

LEE.
why?

RAELYNN.
I don't know
I just do
I think I maybe
I wanna start dressing like
kinda goth?
or like
kinda like Billie Eilish?
she wears those really
she says she wants
I don't know

    beat

LEE.
what are you even talking about

RAELYNN.
I don't know

LEE.
that's not you

RAELYNN.
no but
yeah
I think I might want it to be

LEE.
but you look so pretty without makeup
you don't need it
I hate that shit anyway

RAELYNN.
…
you literally haven't seen me without makeup since we were twelve
you know that, right?
like
my mom taught me how to do my face before she taught me about my period

4.

> *later the same day*
> *after school*
> *feminism club*
> *Raelynn, Beth, and Nell sit in silence for a moment*

NELL.
I mean
should we maybe go ahead and get started?

BETH.
I just kind of feel like we should wait for Mr. Smith

RAELYNN.
he's only the sponsor
he doesn't have to be a part of everything
Ms. Lerner is like never there for key club

BETH.
yeah but he's really excited about being involved
and he took a pretty big chance on us
I don't want him to feel like we don't value that

> *Raelynn rolls her eyes*

I'm *serious*!

RAELYNN.
yeah no I don't really ever like
doubt your seriousness

BETH.
did Ivy text you back?

RAELYNN.
nope

BETH.
me either
it's so weird

we were both trying for perfect attendance this year and she was *just* sick so it's not that

RAELYNN.
yeah

BETH.
(to Raelynn)
are you okay?

RAELYNN.
yeah

    beat

BETH.
you sure?

RAELYNN.
yeah!
why!

NELL.
you've just been
off
today
like in class you seemed / like

RAELYNN.
I mean you barely know me
so I don't know if you know when I'm off

NELL.
wow
okay
sorry I guess

    beat

RAELYNN.
sorry
I didn't mean that

I'm tired

NELL.
k

>*beat*

RAELYNN.
do you think I should have sex with Lee?

>*beat*

NELL.
I just think like
no
right?
yeah
no

BETH.
I mean like have you even been listening to Mr. Smith? and your DAD? about abstinence?

NELL.
Beth you are so confusing sometimes

BETH.
what?

NELL.
this is a feminism club
our bodies, our choices, right?

BETH.
well yeah
but in my head it's also kind of a Christian feminist club

NELL.
I don't really remember that being written into the mission

BETH.
I mean we all go to church together
and that definitely makes us see things in a different—

wait
(to Nell)
where do you go to church?

NELL.
sometimes I go with my dad down in Atlanta
but my mom's not so into it since we moved up here

BETH.
you can come with us to first baptist if you want!
Rae's dad is the preacher
and Mr. Smith goes there too
he and his wife are like
they're so amazing
(to Raelynn)
remember when they did their joint testimony?

RAELYNN.
yeah no it was really amazing
I mean

> *she holds up her hand to show a promise ring on her finger*

I took the Purity Pledge and not just because of my dad
I know people do it and then they change their minds and it's like
whatever for them
but I don't know
I feel really intense and weird about it
maybe I'm being
I mean it had been seven years
that's like almost half our lives

NELL.
whoa
time is crazy

RAELYNN.
exactly!
so yeah!
I still just
I don't know

I feel like maybe I've been overthinking stuff
maybe I should just do it
I don't know

>*beat*

NELL.
do you
want to?

RAELYNN.
yeah!
yeah
of course
yes
but I
I mean yeah!
it's just
it's complicated
I don't know why

BETH.
because it's *sex*

RAELYNN.
(to Nell)
have you had sex?

NELL.
not yet
some makeouts
some hand stuff

RAELYNN.
yeah I mean Lee and I have done *some* stuff

BETH.
Ivy's done stuff too

RAELYNN.
more stuff than me

BETH.
especially when we were in drama oh my god
and Shelby—
…
sorry
…
I haven't had my first kiss yet but I'm okay with it

NELL.
but also?
you answered the question like I asked you
"are you *willing* to have sex with him"
but the question is actually like
do you *want* to have sex with him?

RAELYNN.
the answer is still yes

NELL.
Beth

BETH.
…yes?

NELL.
do you want to have sex with Harry Styles?

> *Beth immediately starts laughing in this really loud, unhinged way*
> *her hands do Not know what to do*

BETH.
I don't know!!!
I mean that's just totally unrealistic to even think about!!!!

NELL.
see?
that's what it looks like to want sex

BETH.
what?????

no!!!!
that's not
I am saving myself for marriage!!!

NELL.
what's that?
you can't stop thinking about Harry's dreamy British dick?

BETH.
ohmygodSTOP
that is disgusting

Beth covers her ears

NELL.
I think maybe
another follow-up question I have
is do you want to have sex with *Lee*?
because it's really two different questions:
do you want to have sex?
and do you want to have sex with *Lee*?

RAELYNN.
who else would I want to have sex with?

NELL.
like literally anyone in the world
Harry Styles
Taylor Swift…

RAELYNN.
I mean if I was going to with any pop star it would be Selena Gomez
but this is dumb
we should get started

Beth looks at Raelynn like Wait a Minute

BETH.
any pop star?

RAELYNN.
any *female* pop star you know what I mean I mean like if I *had* to I thought that was / the question

BETH.
wait is that why you don't want to with Lee?
because you want to with Selena Gomez?

RAELYNN.
I don't *want* to I was just *saying*
it was just an example
I don't want to talk about this anymore!!
if we're gonna meet, let's frickin meet!

> *a moment*
> *then Beth takes out an enormous binder*
> *she is Very Prepared*

BETH.
well I was thinking for today / we could—

> *Beth is interrupted by the classroom door opening*
> *they all look up*
> *Shelby walks in*

SHELBY.
oh

> *they all stare at her*
> *she stares back*
> *a <u>very</u> long silence*

surprise bitch

RAELYNN.
…??
what??
is that all you can say?

SHELBY.
no!
I was trying to be Emma Roberts in *Coven*!

you know
American Horror Story season whatever?
we watched it together?
it's when she comes back from the dead?
it's like
"surprise!"
and now it's that gif?
she's in the red dress?
anyway
it was the first thing I thought of
I don't know why
it's stupid
don't look at me
…
so I'm looking for Principal David
the secretary said to check hall C
he's gotta sign a form since I'm coming back
because yeah so fyi
I'm coming back

    beat

BETH.
we signed out the room
he must be somewhere else

RAELYNN.
we started a feminism club

SHELBY.
weird

RAELYNN.
what's that supposed to mean?

SHELBY.
I mean not weird
unexpected?
I don't know
I just

said it

>*beat*

NELL.
I'm Nell

SHELBY.
hey
Shelby

NELL.
ohhhhh

SHELBY.
yeah
That Shelby

BETH.
Nell moved from Atlanta

SHELBY.
oh cool I was just in Atlanta
it's like we switched places

NELL.
what were you doing there?

SHELBY.
taking a sabbatical
that's what my aunt Susan called it

RAELYNN.
what does that even mean?
you're not jewish

SHELBY.
um
I think you're thinking of the Sabbath
sabbatical is different
it means like I took a break
basically

RAELYNN.
there was already Christmas break built in
how many breaks do you need?

BETH.
sabbaticals are actually for college professors to pursue their research

NELL.
oh Beth

BETH.
well they are!!

> *Beth's phone dings*
> *she unlocks it and reads*
> *she covers her mouth*

RAELYNN.
we were just about to get started
so
yeah

BETH.
(still looking at her phone)
oh no

NELL.
what

BETH.
oh my god
you guys
oh my god

> *they all crowd around her to look at the phone, except Shelby*
> *beat*

NELL.
holy shit

SHELBY.
what?

RAELYNN.
oh my god

BETH.
what do I even *say*?

> *Raelynn grabs her own phone and texts*

SHELBY.
what??
tell me!
my parents took away my phone

NELL.
it's a text from Ivy

BETH.
her dad is like
his secretary or I guess she's not his secretary anymore
she's saying that like
stuff
happened
between them
I mean
not good stuff
in like
a not good way

> *beat*

RAELYNN.
this is insane

NELL.
did y'all know his secretary?

RAELYNN.
kind of

BETH.
she's Addi's cousin, right?

SHELBY.
no she used to go out with Addi's brother

RAELYNN.
she's not from here

BETH.
that's right
she's from Hewitt

NELL.
isn't that just like
ten minutes away, though?
where the walmart is?

BETH.
we should do something for Ivy
make sure she knows we're like
there for her family

NELL.
so you think it's not true?

> *beat*
> *they all look at Nell*

I just mean you know
I don't know her dad
so I wasn't / sure if

SHELBY.
I mean
I'm not really like
Surprised by it

> *Raelynn and Beth look at Shelby in shock*

RAELYNN.
what
is your problem

SHELBY.
no it's just like
he always does those weird massages
right?
like at sleepovers?
you know what I'm talking about

NELL.
jesus

BETH.
no, it's not—
he's just being nice

RAELYNN.
he's affectionate

BETH.
he's a *dad*

SHELBY.
yeah
a gross dad who stands behind us
and frickin rubs our shoulders while we're in pajamas

RAELYNN.
don't make this into something it's not

SHELBY.
Rae
come on
we had this whole conversation about it when we were like thirteen
it's weird

RAELYNN.
we talked about a lot of things when we were thirteen
we're not thirteen anymore

    beat

SHELBY.
whatever

I bet his secretary isn't the only one
like I'd actually bet
I'd put money on it

RAELYNN.
this is Ivy's *life*
you're being such a dick

SHELBY.
yeah
probably

RAELYNN.
weren't you gonna go find Principal David?

BETH.
Mr. Smith might know where he is
he should be back soon
he's our sponsor

SHELBY.
why are you in this room instead of his?

BETH.
yeah they actually switched some of the rooms over Christmas
so Mr. Smith's in here now

> *Shelby looks around the room*

SHELBY.
weird

> *Beth takes something from Mr. Smith's desk – a framed picture*
> *she hands it to Shelby*

BETH.
and look!!
they're gonna have a baby!
isn't that the best news ever??

RAELYNN.
they found out while you were gone

SHELBY.
nice
"like sands through the hourglass"

RAELYNN.
what?

SHELBY.
nothing
…
well
Principal David awaits

>　*then she leaves*
>　*beat*

BETH.
(to Raelynn)
you okay?

RAELYNN.
yeah
no
I mean
…
…
that was so weird
like
she walked in
and for a minute I was just
really happy to see her

BETH.
yeah

NELL.
wait so
did she go to Atlanta because of you and Lee?

like
was that the only reason?

BETH.
no one really knows
my mom thinks she must've like
had a breakdown
like
gone crazy or something

RAELYNN.
maybe she didn't "go" crazy
because she's always been crazy

BETH.
she's just intense

RAELYNN.
you literally just said she went crazy

BETH.
my *mom* said that

NELL.
you did like
repeat it though

BETH.
well sorry

NELL.
I mean
she does seem
I dunno

RAELYNN.
she's a Lot

BETH.
yeah…
she kind of always has been

beat

NELL.
that's funny
my family says stuff like that about me all the time
like my mom says it to my aunt on the phone like I can't hear, she's like
"Nell's just a lot"
"Nell is so dramatic these days"
"Nell is too much for me right now"
I dunno like
I think it's just
when people say stuff like that
they always kinda mean the same thing
you know?
like what they really mean is just
"Nell's a girl"

beat

BETH.
whoa

NELL.
I dunno

BETH.
we should come back to this idea
I'll put it in the minutes

RAELYNN.
are you the secretary too?
on top of being president?

BETH.
do you wanna take notes?

RAELYNN.
not / really

BETH.
yeah
so
yeah

> *Beth takes some notes*
> *then all of a sudden, Nell has a Major Realization*

NELL.
wait
you guys
wait

BETH.
what??

NELL.
I just thought of something and maybe it's crazy but maybe it's not
and I just
okay…
do you think something
Happened
with Shelby and Ivy's dad…?

> *beat*

BETH.
what do you mean?

NELL.
I mean like
the way she was just acting? when we all found out?
she literally said she wasn't surprised
and she kinda seemed to get upset??
and then she said that thing like "I bet the secretary isn't the only one" I mean
I don't know I just
I know I don't know her

BETH.
oh
my god

> *the classroom door opens again*
> *Mr. Smith comes in with Mason*
> *Beth stands up for some reason and immediately feels so dumb and weird about it*

MR. SMITH.
ladies
I got a new recruit for ya!

MASON.
hey

BETH.
hi!!!

MR. SMITH.
so Mason
these girls are changing the world
the future is female

NELL.
actually, that's kind of problematic

BETH.
the future exists outside of binaries

RAELYNN.
the future is intersectional

MR. SMITH.
see?
I learn something new in here every meeting
I'm running to a quick faculty meeting now
but when I get back, hit me with everything you got

> *he leaves*
> *a long pause*

Mason chooses a desk
he kind of puts his head down

RAELYNN.
has um
do you not have basketball practice?

MASON.
what?
oh
yeah I'm just kind of failing some stuff
so Mr. Smith is helping me get extra credit
he said y'all are gonna make this about that play
and we didn't make playoffs anyway so it's whatever

> *beat*

RAELYNN.
cool

MASON.
yeah y'all don't mind me
I'm just
here

5.

two days later
before school
Miss Gallagher and Mr. Smith

MISS GALLAGHER.
thank you for doing this
I know it's early

MR. SMITH.
of course

MISS GALLAGHER.
I just really want to set her up for success
you know?
from her file at least it seems like she's always been one of the tricky ones

MR. SMITH.
there's a lot going on in there
I really think she's got potential

MISS GALLAGHER.
I think so too!
and just so you know what you're walking into
this was not a prolonged absence that went through any um proper channels
we don't know a lot about why she was gone, but her parents thought this was their only option, based on some of Shelby's um concerning behavior

MR. SMITH.
right

MISS GALLAGHER.
so we're approaching the reentry very delicately
everything's just so crazy lately—
you know, with the mayor
and now Ivy Watkins's father

all these stories
I just want to make her feel supported and safe

MR. SMITH.
I love that you're actually trying to do your job

MISS GALLAGHER.
well I
of course

MR. SMITH.
it's not "of course"
it's really not
you know?
I've seen other people in your position just keep their heads down and fill out whatever paperwork it takes to get half our seniors into college

MISS GALLAGHER.
I just want to be
I don't know
better than that
I guess

MR. SMITH.
well I think that's just so great

MISS GALLAGHER.
well thanks

>   *they smile at each other*
>   *beat*

MR. SMITH.
hold on
sorry
my memory is terrible
we weren't in school at the same time, right?

MISS GALLAGHER.
no

no I'm
I think I'm like eight years? younger than you?
somethin like that

MR. SMITH.
right

MISS GALLAGHER.
my brother was a couple years below you, though
y'all played basketball together

MR. SMITH.
right!
Chip!
I can't believe I don't remember hanging around you more
ol' Chip and I were thick as thieves there for a while

MISS GALLAGHER.
yeah I guess he
well he's uh mellowed out a little
but he was always real overprotective back then
with me and boys

MR. SMITH.
classic big brother

MISS GALLAGHER.
yeah plus you were older
you know
it doesn't make a big difference now, but
it did then

MR. SMITH.
for sure

MISS GALLAGHER.
I guess it didn't help that I always kind of had a little bit of a crush on you

MR. SMITH.
is that right

MISS GALLAGHER.
back when I was in middle school
forever ago
not anymore

> *a loaded beat*

MR. SMITH.
so you're doin okay?
first year and all?
it's a doozy

MISS GALLAGHER.
oh
yeah
no
it's fine

MR. SMITH.
I mean ten years in and I feel like I'm definitely still figuring it out too
but I can help
if you want
you can always come to me

MISS GALLAGHER.
that's really really nice
thank you
I will

> *a knock at the door*
> *Shelby peeks her head in*

SHELBY.
hey
sorry I'm late

MISS GALLAGHER.
Shelby!
come on in!

MR. SMITH.
Shelby, it's good to have you back

SHELBY.
it's good to be back

MISS GALLAGHER.
thanks so much for takin the time before school
I know you're a busy girl

SHELBY.
yeah no it's
yeah it's no problem

MISS GALLAGHER.
I just think it's good to start back on the same page after a prolonged absence
see how you're doing

SHELBY.
I'm good

MISS GALLAGHER.
good
good
and you know
make sure you had a chance to check in with all your teachers individually
ask any questions before your first day

SHELBY.
yeah def
mos def mos def
not the rapper mos def
no offense to him he's great
he's an actor too
very compelling presence
sorry
I'm a little nervous

MISS GALLAGHER.
oh no!

SHELBY.
no no it's fine!
it's not for any like
particular reason
it's just weird being back
I feel like I
I dunno
I mean I hardly ever leave here?
my family doesn't even like go to the beach or whatever so
I went with Ivy's family one summer to their house in Destin but I never went back

    beat

MISS GALLAGHER.
I know exactly what you mean
have you had a chance to reconnect with your friends?

SHELBY.
oh yeah
saw 'em all the other day
the whole gang
plus the new girl
well Ivy wasn't there because of her
yeah

MISS GALLAGHER.
oh
oh yes that's a very
it's
well
I'm sure they were happy to see you

    beat

I gave Mr. Smith your makeup work

MR. SMITH.
I haven't had a chance to look at it yet
but I'm not worried
you've always done great work in my classes

SHELBY.
okay cool
thank you

MR. SMITH.
and you're all caught up on *The Crucible*?

SHELBY.
yeah I actually finished the whole thing, I couldn't put it down

MR. SMITH.
you're back just in time, we'll assign partners for the interpretive project today

SHELBY.
the movie came on tv like a million years ago and Daniel Day-Lewis was super hot as the main guy

…
so um
is there anything
is everything else good?

MISS GALLAGHER.
if you're good, we're good

SHELBY.
I'm good

MR. SMITH.
and if you have any problems, Shelby
getting back in the rhythm of things
we can pair you with a student-tutor, find you some extra credit
whatever you need

SHELBY.
oh! Mr. Smith!

sorry, I forgot I—
Beth told me the good news!
congratulations!
on your baby!

MR. SMITH.
oh thank you!
that's so sweet of you to mention

SHELBY.
you're gonna be such great parents
you must be really excited

MR. SMITH.
we really are
thank you so much

SHELBY.
when is she due?

MR. SMITH.
this summer
july

SHELBY.
cancer or leo
pretty big gamble
but I'm partial to fire signs myself
aries aries sag[*]
triple fire
huge surprise

MR. SMITH.
we missed you, Shelby
welcome back

---

[*] soft g (short for sagittarius)

6.

>*later the same day, class*
>*Ivy's back*
>*they're reading from* The Crucible
>*Shelby's a great reader – she's not afraid to really Go There*

IVY.
(as Betty)
"You drank blood, Abby! You didn't tell him that!"

SHELBY.
(as Abigail)
"Betty, you never say that again! You will never—"

IVY.
(as Betty)
"You did, you did! You drank a charm to kill John Proctor's wife! You drank a charm to kill Goody Proctor!"

>*tiny beat*
>*they look to Mason*

MASON.
oh sorry
uh
I forget
do I still read them if it's in her line like that?

MR. SMITH.
yes please

MASON.
(reading stage directions)
"Abigail, smashes her across the face"

LEE.
dude!

SHELBY.
(as Abigail)

"Shut it! Now shut it!"

MASON.
(reading stage directions)
"Betty, collapsing on the bed"

IVY.
(as Betty)
"Mama, Mama!"

MASON.
(reading stage directions)
"She dissolves into sobs."

> *and then Ivy actually does dissolve into sobs*
> *it feels like she's probably been holding this in for days*

BETH.
are you okay?

> *Ivy runs out of the room*
> *a beat*
> *nobody really knows what to do*
> *so then Shelby keeps going*
> *she gets Really Intense during this next monologue*
> *by the end, she's unhinged and kinda scary*

SHELBY.
(as Abigail)
"Now look you. All of you. We danced. And Tituba conjured Ruth Putnam's dead sisters. And that is all. And mark this. Let either of you breathe a word, or the edge of a word, about the other things, and I will come to you in the black of some terrible night and I will bring a pointy reckoning that will shudder you. And you know I can do it; I saw Indians smash my dear parents' heads on the pillow next to mine, and I have seen some reddish work done at night, and I can make you wish you had never seen the sun go down!"

> *beat*

BETH.
Mason

MASON.
shit
I mean
sorry

> *Ivy comes back in, embarrassed*

MR. SMITH.
no no it's okay
why don't we stop there for now
we're running out of time
sorry, Mary Warren

BETH.
(disappointed)
oh
it's okay

MR. SMITH.
that was awesome, everybody
really well done
and thanks to Shelby
for volunteering to jump in there with Abigail on her first day back
so tell me
what's notable about this scene

> *tiny beat*
> *Beth raises her hand*

BETH.
I mean
sorry
they admit they've done witchcraft
right?

MR. SMITH.
right!
and why do you think they would do witchcraft in the first place?

they had to know how severe the consequences would be if they got caught
why did they go and dance naked in the woods?

    beat

LEE.
for fun?

MR. SMITH.
interesting
could you expand on that thought a little bit?

LEE.
um
I dunno
it just seems like maybe they were bored

MR. SMITH.
that's a great observation, Lee
because one interesting thing about Salem during this time
is the fact that there was no entertainment

MASON.
so kinda like here

MR. SMITH.
actually no
we might have to drive thirty minutes to the mall
but they didn't even have music in church
they were still waiting on a ship to bring over a piano
I know it was the olden days so you're probably thinking "okay Mr. Smith we get it"
but it's hard for us to imagine how isolated it was

    Beth raises her hand

BETH.
I also read that most of the girls had lost their fathers

MR. SMITH.
yes
that's true
many men died in attacks on the new villages

LEE.
indian attacks?

BETH.
we don't say "indian" anymore

LEE.
who's "we"?

BETH.
the world
I mean
sorry

LEE.
yeah dude it's like
Abigail says it right there in the play
I'm just quoting the play

Shelby raises her hand

SHELBY.
I also think like
I think probably
they went out dancing
because it was like
the only way to *deal* with everything
you know?

MR. SMITH.
"everything" meaning what?

SHELBY.
um
like
their lives?

just
yeah no yeah
their lives

NELL.
exactly
I mean people still do that, right?
they go out dancing to like blow off steam

MR. SMITH.
absolutely
that's a great connection, both of you
I'm sure it felt good to get away from their daily lives
they were under a lot of pressure

he checks his watch

okay y'all we're almost out of time
so they went dancing in the woods
they got caught
then what happens?

NELL.
they start saying that everybody else is a witch instead of them

MR. SMITH.
yes!
and why would they do that?
purely self-preservation, or something more?

RAELYNN.
it's like
the more we say something the less we
or like the less the thing we say is
I don't know what I'm trying to
yeah
no

STUDENT (or MASON).
yeah

MR. SMITH.
I kind of think of it like the boy who cried wolf
who knows what I mean by that?

LEE.
sometimes girls just make stuff up

STUDENT (or BETH).
it's the *boy* who cried wolf

LEE.
I was talking about the girls in *The Crucible*
calm down

STUDENT (or NELL).
riiiight

LEE.
you callin me a liar?

MR. SMITH.
no matter *who* makes things up—
boys, girls, teenagers, adults—
one lie can poison the entire well of truth
but let's dig a little deeper—
what did these girls stand to gain?

NELL.
I mean it's all kind of about power

RAELYNN.
yeah because they had none
right?

BETH.
like less than none

MR. SMITH.
awesome
yes
I think you're all right on the money

LEE.
but Abigail wants to kill the wife of the dude she was with so she can keep bangin him

MASON.
wait
is there sex in *The Crucible*?

LEE.
so I don't know if it's this whole feminist empowerment thing like y'all think

NELL.
but I mean sex is power
so there's definitely a connection there

MASON.
(thumbing through his book)
I feel like I'm reading a completely different play
I thought *The Crucible* was about witches

7.

>*later the same day*
>*after school*

IVY.
it sucks
which like
that sounds dumb to say
because obviously
but yeah
it's been really really bad

RAELYNN.
how's your mom?

IVY.
I've like
hardly seen her?
she's just
in her room a lot

BETH.
she made that whole statement, though

IVY.
yeah no
that was basically just the lawyer
I don't really know if it's even true

RAELYNN.
what does your dad say?

IVY.
I mean he says it's not true
so yeah
or like
I guess he says that he did
touch her?
or whatever?

but like
the way he touches everybody
and I guess she just misunderstood?
I mean
you guys know my dad
he's just nice
he's just really nice to everybody
and she doesn't even work for him anymore
he got her this really great job down in Kennesaw
so why would she even take a job my dad got her if he's this terrible person??
but yeah
he's been like sleeping in my brother's old room
it's really
…
…
look
I don't know if I feel good about doing this anymore
like
(gestures to all of them)
this

BETH.
feminism club?

IVY.
yeah
it's just
I think Miss Gallagher was right
it's not a good / time

NELL.
but like
what does being a feminist have to do with your dad?

IVY.
I mean I feel like the only reason this is even a thing
is because all of a sudden Me Too stuff is just everywhere
you know?

like even my grandpa knows about Harvey Weinstein
and my grandpa doesn't know anything about anything past like 1990

BETH.
but like
sorry
but it's not really all of a sudden?
like at all?
I mean Tarana Burke started Me Too in 2006
it's just
people weren't listening until now

IVY.
but it's not just like
I mean these are people's *dads*
you know?
I feel like I wasn't thinking about it like that before
how would you feel if it was *your* dad?

beat

RAELYNN.
Ivy's right
it does feel really different now
it feels like
I don't know
it feels different

IVY.
yeah it's all just so much
I mean that's why *The Crucible* made me lose it in class it like
my dad even said this whole thing feels like a witch hunt
I don't know I feel like I'm not making sense
I know we're trying to do good stuff and be good feminists
Beth, I know we made all these plans
but we also don't wanna give the wrong impression

BETH.
then we won't

IVY.
it's really messed up that you're not supporting me right now
my dad was your frickin tee-ball coach!
you're my best friend!

RAELYNN.
Ivy, we love you
we're here for you

BETH.
I'm sorry, Ivy
I love your dad
I love you so much
I

>*the classroom door opens*
>*Mason comes in, with Lee*

MASON.
sup
sorry I'm late
but I brought Lee
male feminists, motherfucker!!

>*Ivy leaves*

MASON.
oh shit was she crying again

NELL.
you don't have to say *male* feminist, you know
it's just feminist

LEE.
but "fem" is in the word
and that means girl
right?

BETH.
well
technically yes, but—

Mason and Lee high-five

MASON.
nailed it!

BETH.
but STILL

    beat

LEE.
(re Ivy)
sucks about her dad

NELL.
yeah

MASON.
messed up

BETH.
yeah

MASON.
how many is it?

NELL.
how many women?

LEE.
it's just the one, right?

RAELYNN.
I mean I feel like "just" is maybe not like
the right word

BETH.
there was another one in the paper this morning but it hasn't been
like verified

    beat

RAELYNN.
I'm gonna go check on her

LEE.
do you need help?

RAELYNN.
…
why would I need help?

> *Raelynn leaves*
> *pause*

LEE.
so what do y'all do in this club

BETH.
well
we talk about feminist issues

NELL.
we try to fill the gaps of our lacking education

BETH.
it's still really new
we've kinda gotten
derailed
with
you know
everything

MASON.
but no dude
it's really cool
they've been teaching me a lot of stuff

NELL.
you've only been to like
one-and-a-half meetings

MASON.
yeah but
I dunno
that's more than none

beat

BETH.
yeah so before you got here
Ivy was kind of talking about how she like
I dunno she maybe doesn't want to do this anymore?
so I think we're just kinda
figuring out what to do next

MASON.
oh okay
I mean that sucks
Ivy's hot
but whatever
we can still meet without her

NELL.
no like she doesn't think we should have a club at all

MASON.
wait
nooooo
dude
I really need the extra credit

LEE.
so does that mean
is it true about Shelby and Ivy's dad?

MASON.
yeah like is she gonna be the next girl to say something about him?

NELL.
(to Beth)
did you tell them what I said?

BETH.
what?? no!!

NELL.
where did you hear that?

Lee shrugs

MASON.
I mean
I've heard it from like five people

LEE.
yeah Raelynn told me like
back in eighth grade or something that Shelby was creeped out by him
I kinda figured that was why she was acting so weird
something must have happened before she left

NELL.
you mean the whole thing with you wasn't enough?

MASON.
oh burn

LEE.
(to Nell)
dude you like
weren't even here
you don't know what happened

NELL.
I didn't have to be here to know you're an asshole
that's clear like right away

BETH.
okay you guys
we don't have / to do this

MASON.
I wonder who was better
you or Ivy's dad

BETH.
MASON!!!!

MASON.
sorry

beat

BETH.
well
we had a Very Full agenda set for today
but it doesn't feel like we're going to accomplish much now

NELL.
yeah we kind of need everybody here to plan the bake sale

LEE.
don't feminists want to like
not cook and stuff?

NELL.
that's an oversimplification

MASON.
and it's a bake sale to raise money for Planned Parenthood

BETH.
yeah so meeting adjourned I guess
but just fyi we were gonna talk about the problematic way white feminism is monopolizing the mainstream body positivity movement which is really important and thank god for Lizzo but also she's just one person and one person can't be everything to everyone and I found a great article about it so I guess I'm just gonna stay here and read for as long as we have the room
anyone is welcome to join me
I made worksheets

8.

> *early the next week*
> *Shelby and Raelynn work on their project*
> *the same classroom, before school*
> *long silence*

SHELBY.
we don't have to make it a thing

> *Raelynn stares*

I just mean that we can make it so we both like
come up with different stuff
and put it together
and don't even have to talk to each other much

RAELYNN.
he always knows when people do that
that's not the point of collaboration

SHELBY.
he had to have done this on purpose, right?

RAELYNN.
I don't think he knows

SHELBY.
I think all the teachers know more than we think they do

RAELYNN.
we literally watched him draw the names
you sound a little crazy

SHELBY.
cool
thanks

> *Raelynn unfolds a piece of paper and reads from it*

RAELYNN.
"choose any two characters from *The Crucible* who never have a scene alone together and imagine what this scene might be. what would they say? what do they need from each other? create a performance no longer than five minutes long, based on this scene and incorporating at least two outside sources. your scene should—"
(stops reading from the paper)
blah blah blah blah
basically just "make it good"
so I guess maybe we should start by reading the play

SHELBY.
I already did

RAELYNN.
(sure you did)
right
okay

SHELBY.
why would you just assume I haven't read the play?

RAELYNN.
well I know you

SHELBY.
I guess you don't
I literally did research on the play
I read a book
I showed up before school for this
I make a lot of fucking effort
but you're acting like I'm the same Shelby who copied your homework in sixth grade
and like
I fucked up with you
I know that
but that doesn't mean I Always fuck up
and just because I like
let you see things about me that other people don't see

doesn't mean that you get to use those things against me
I

>*Raelynn covers her face with her hands, crying*

hey
no no no no don't cry
heyyy
I'm sorry
I'm sorry I'm sorry I'm sorry

>*pause*
>*Raelynn keeps her face covered*

I really want to hug you
and I feel like maybe it's not a good idea
but I really want to

>*beat*

Rae?

>*Shelby gingerly puts a hand on Raelynn's shoulder*
>*Raelynn lets her*
>*a moment, during which Shelby starts crying a little*
>*Raelynn peeks at her then jerks her hands away from her face*

RAELYNN.
why are *you* crying??

SHELBY.
because!!

RAELYNN.
you yelled at *me*!!

SHELBY.
there's just a lot, okay!!
there's just a lot

>*they look at each other for a moment, tearful*

hey
so I really want / to say

RAELYNN.
let's just
we really need to work on this do you have any ideas?

>*beat*

SHELBY.
I mean
I feel like we both know we're gonna do a dance

>*Raelynn laughs automatically, against her will*

RAELYNN.
I mean yeah obviously

SHELBY.
we've been waiting our whole lives for an assignment with "interpretive" in the title for this very reason
we're very gifted very beautiful interpretive dancers

>*Shelby does a little bit of a cheesy interpretive dance*
>*Raelynn hesitates, then riffs on Shelby with her own version*
>*they laugh*
>*they love each other so much*
>*there are miles to go, but they're testing the ground, inching toward fixing this*
>*beat*

RAELYNN.
now what?

SHELBY.
you tell me

9.

> *later the same day*
> *Beth eats lunch in Mr. Smith's classroom*
> *she reads quietly while he grades papers*

BETH.
thanks for letting me do this

MR. SMITH.
Beth, you always have a place here
you don't have to say thank you every time

BETH.
okay
sorry
thank you

MR. SMITH.
I should really be thanking *you* for the good company

> *Beth beams*
> *beat*

BETH.
um so I've been thinking a lot about *The Great Gatsby*

MR. SMITH.
I knew you'd love it

BETH.
but like in the context of Lorde and *Melodrama*?
do you know Lorde?

MR. SMITH.
I know my lord and savior jesus christ

BETH.
oh no I
she's a singer

MR. SMITH.
I'm kidding
I know who you're talking about
I'm not that old

BETH.
sorry!!
okay well she has all this commentary on party culture like throughout her body of work which totally lines up with *Gatsby*
but the main thing I've been thinking about is the song "Green Light" you know?

MR. SMITH.
(singing badly, on purpose)
"that green light, I want it"

BETH.
oh my god??

MR. SMITH.
see?
I know all the cool things

> *Beth laughs but also melts into the ground from sheer embarrassment*

BETH.
I'm going to pretend you didn't just do that
anyway...
it's interesting because in the context of the song
a green light is kinda like permission? to move on?
or like that's how I interpret it like she wants to move on
which is obviously the connotation at like stoplights or whatever
but in the book the green light is like this concrete image of Gatsby *never* moving on and his like inability to realize the American dream, like he's stuck in these ideas
so it's just a
yeah I'm just thinking about the different meanings I guess
like as symbolism

MR. SMITH.
or maybe
Lorde was never using it like a stoplight at all
maybe she wants her ex to leave the metaphoric green light on for her
just like Gatsby
it seems like there's a commonality there—
youth, parties, longing…
maybe Lorde is absolutely conscious of that reference

BETH.
…
oh
my god
you totally just blew my mind

MR. SMITH.
it's just an idea

BETH.
no it's great it's I love it I want to write about it I
you're the best teacher I've ever had

>   *a half knock on the door*
>   *it's Shelby*

SHELBY.
hey
sorry
Beth?
I was just in the library?
are you still good / to—?

BETH.
oh no I'm so sorry I completely forgot!!!

SHELBY.
no that's fine
we can do it another time / or something

BETH.
no no no!!
now's great!
(to Mr. Smith)
I'm helping Shelby get caught up in history
Miss Gallagher said I can list it as tutoring for college

MR. SMITH.
that's great, girls
it's a win-win

BETH.
(to Shelby)
sorry
I just came to eat in here to get away from like
I mean I've been having kind of a tough time with Ivy's dad and everything?
sorry to / like

SHELBY.
yeah no totally

MR. SMITH.
you know you two are welcome to stay in here
if you don't wanna go to the library
I won't bother you

BETH.
that's perfect!
(to Shelby)
we were just talking about "Green Light"

SHELBY.
you mean the best song of all time?

BETH.
yeah like in conversation with *The Great Gatsby*!

SHELBY.
naturally

BETH.
Mr. Smith has this interpretation that's just like
brain-exploding
wait oh my god do you remember the day it came out?

SHELBY.
oh my god at your house?

BETH.
Mr. Smith, last year when it came out we sat on my floor
and played this song on repeat for literally like two hours straight
just sitting and like

SHELBY.
listening

BETH.
and then we had a dance party that got so intense
Raelynn cried and Ivy almost threw up

Shelby laughs

SHELBY.
I forgot about that

BETH.
(a performative look toward an invisible horizon)
"was anyone ever so young?"

SHELBY.
(smokes a fake cigarette)
 "I am here to tell you that someone was."

they both laugh

MR. SMITH.
I hate to break it to ya, but you're both still pretty young

BETH.
sorry that's—
it's from a Joan Didion essay?
it's just like a

thing we do
sorry

SHELBY.
it's our little bit
it's weird
we're weird

MR. SMITH.
Beth, I love that you love Joan Didion
Slouching Towards Bethlehem is one of my favorites

BETH.
Shelby actually introduced me to her

SHELBY.
yeah
Beth isn't the only one who reads
I think Walt Whitman probably said it best:
I contain frickin multitudes

10.

> *later the same day*
> *class*
> *folks are a bit rowdy*

MR. SMITH.
okay okay
enough of that
it's *Crucible* o'clock

> *groans and laughter*

I cannot wait to see what y'all are cookin up for those interpretive projects
they'll be here before you know it
anyway
it felt like we got into some great stuff around power last week with acts one and two and now that we've read through the end I'd love to circle back to the girls' motivation

SHELBY.
I was / reading this—

BETH.
I did a little bit of
oh
sorry
I didn't mean to interrupt you

SHELBY.
no go ahead

BETH.
okay so I did a little bit of research
and the girls were largely used as pawns by the town officials
to settle land disputes

MR. SMITH.
Beth's right
the town of Salem / was very—

SHELBY.
I mean I also did some research
sorry but like the thing that nobody in this play is talking about
is that pretty much all these girls had been like
assaulted at some point
I mean like
sexually

> *gasps and murmurs*
> *Ivy is especially horrified*

MR. SMITH.
all right, Shelby let's tone it down a little
be considerate

SHELBY.
no but those are just facts!
I read this book that says most of these girls probably had like PTSD
which explains the like crazy physical fits that people thought were happening because of witchcraft but anyway so yeah like the assault stuff was *everywhere*
their dads
older men in the town
stable boys
whoever
and even if you managed to get by without *that* happening—
even then you'd probably lost your dad
like Beth said the other day
and so it / was like

IVY.
what are you trying to say?

SHELBY.
what?
no /
nothing

IVY.
I mean
sexual stuff
dads
it sounds like you want to say something to me

MR. SMITH.
okay ladies
let's take / a minute

SHELBY.
no I only brought up dads / to say they all died!

MR. SMITH.
Shelby
let's just—

SHELBY.
and like in really violent crazy ways
like scalpings and guttings and stuff

MASON.
indian attacks!!

NELL.
oh my / GOD

RAELYNN.
Mason

MASON.
sorry

MR. SMITH.
Miss Holcomb
those are really
fascinating points
but I'm going to have to ask you to keep it to the text

SHELBY.
why doesn't Beth have to keep it to the text?

and I *am* keeping it to the text, Abigail literally has that whole monologue about watching her parents' heads get split open

MR. SMITH.
speaking of Beth's point from earlier
it does beg the larger question—
do we think the girls knew they were being used to settle land disputes?
were they puppets or were they complicit?

SHELBY.
maybe not all the girls knew
but Abigail was like clearly super smart

STUDENT (or IVY).
she was clearly crazy

BETH.
let's be careful about calling women "crazy"

STUDENT (or IVY).
but what about women who are crazy?

SHELBY.
but also like
John Proctor never even apologized

BETH.
what does he need to apologize for?

SHELBY.
also he calls Abby a whore like
at least five times

LEE.
she *is* a whore, though

NELL.
but he was the married guy who took her virginity

SHELBY.
and also he was her boss??

NELL.
right?
so like if she's a whore
what is he?

SHELBY.
I think she was awesome

MASON.
awkward

SHELBY.
how is it awkward, Mason?
like
that's not what that word means
do you not know that?
are you stupid?
or are you just fucking annoying?

MASON.
whoa

MR. SMITH.
language, Miss Holcomb

LEE.
you kiss Ivy's dad with that mouth?

MR. SMITH.
(sharper than we've ever heard him)
Lee!
Principal David, now!

> *Lee leaves*
> *everyone's a little shaken*
> *Mr. Smith takes a second*

I'm sorry about that y'all
I really am
I
…

why don't we shift gears a little bit
give ourselves some space from that particular discussion
yeah?
let's jump to the end of the play
no matter what we think about the girls' motivations
at this point the damage is done, right?
and John Proctor is a flawed man, absolutely
that's partly what makes him such a rich dramatic character
but in his last moments, he has the opportunity to live
and he has a lot to live for
he and his wife have just begun to reconcile
their relationship has been torn apart by all this
they have a baby on the way
all he has to do is lie
and he can go back to his life and family
the stakes couldn't be higher
but he would rather die than put that stain on his good name
I'd love if we could read that final monologue
page one hundred and thirty-three*
any volunteers?

> *of course Beth's hand goes up*
> *but surprisingly, so does Mason's*

Mason!
yeah!
"with a cry of his whole soul…"

MASON.
(as John Proctor, stiffly but trying)
"Because it is my name! Because I cannot have another in my life! Because I lie and sign myself to lies! Because I am not worth the dust on the feet of them that hang! How may I live without my name? I have given you my soul; leave me my name!"

> *applause*

---

* or whatever page number it is in your edition

MR. SMITH.
well read, Mason, well read
that's my favorite part of the play
such an incredible monologue

> *Shelby raises her hand*

Shelby!
yeah!
start us off

SHELBY.
I don't get it
all you have is your name?
what is THAT?

BETH.
I think it means that like
Proctor is saying / that he—

SHELBY.
no no yeah I mean I get it
(sparknotes voice)
"this allows him to die, honorably, with his goodness intact"
it says that on sparknotes
but I still feel like
what GOODNESS?

MR. SMITH.
okay well we should talk about your use of sparknotes and how that does not foster a meaningful relationship with the text

SHELBY.
I also read the play
I did!
I just thought I was missing something
so I looked at sparknotes as like supplemental material
anyway I totally get what the monologue is doing from like
a literary standpoint I guess
but your name is literally just a word that someone else gave to you
you can change it

you can give it to someone else—
I mean
you gave yours to your wife
and that's another shitty thing!

MR. SMITH.
language…

NELL.
but right?
women's names are all tied up in their relationship to a man
we were just talking about this in feminism club

MASON.
yeah it's like
women have "miss" and "ms" and "mrs"
and all men have is "mister"
it's kind of fucked up

MR. SMITH.
Mason!
language!

SHELBY.
okay but wait
I have a point, I swear
it's a good one
I make really good points
I'm really smart
I know a lot of you don't think I am, but I am
you've told me I am, Mr. Smith
remember?
I do
I remember it very clearly
I remember exactly where we were

MR. SMITH.
…yes, Shelby, I think you're very smart
I think all of you are smart

and my goal as an educator
is to get you to apply that intelligence / into—

SHELBY.
I mean that's not really how you phrased it to me
but okay
so anyway
it's like
your name was made up
your ancestors were like
"ooh there are a bunch of blacksmiths in our family, better call ourselves Smith"
like that's what names *are*
they're fiction
but my body is a fact
I live inside of it

MR. SMITH.
we're going to have to wrap up this point pretty soon, Miss Holcomb
if you could please bring it back to the text?

SHELBY.
Abigail was a human being
she like
she existed
that's a fact
but John Proctor is just obsessed with this made-up thing

BETH.
yeah but
his name stood for a lot more
it's like
his reputation
his honor

STUDENT (or IVY).
and Abigail's been trying the whole play to like
ruin him

NELL.
nope
he made choices

SHELBY.
exactly!
but he's just pretending like
I dunno like
his fiction is more important than her fact?
I mean
that *sucks*
like
John Proctor is clearly the villain
right?

MR. SMITH.
John Proctor is one of the great heroes of the American Thea/tre

SHELBY.
yeahhhhh no
I don't think he is
I think he sucks

reactions

MR. SMITH.
okay well I think we all have a lot to mull over / and we

SHELBY.
last thing last point I swear
say you run into someone who might not recognize you right away
and they're like
"Mr. Smith? Carter Smith? is that you?"
you could easily be like
"oh no, sorry you must be thinking of someone else, that's not my name"
but if I run into someone and they're like
"are you living inside of a body or are you a ghost?"
I mean I am pretty clearly inside of a body

MR. SMITH.
Shelby, let's / just

SHELBY.
a name doesn't mean anything if it doesn't have a body to be attached to
your name doesn't have a memory, *Carter*
but my body remembers being touched by you
and I know your body remembers mine

> *confused reactions and murmurs from the class*

MR. SMITH.
all right, Shelby
I'm gonna have to ask you to leave
right now

SHELBY.
wow
yeah
it's funny you're asking me to leave
when six months ago
you were asking me to come

> *the class is in shock*
> *this might look like a lot of different things*

11.

one week later
the same classroom
Shelby's gone
Mr. Smith is also gone
Miss Gallagher stands at the front of the room

MISS GALLAGHER.
I appreciate you bearing with me while we get all this sorted out
I know it's been a
tough week
but we
things should be back to normal soon

NELL.
what does that mean?

STUDENT (or RAELYNN).
is Mr. Smith coming back?

MISS GALLAGHER.
it means
that we're working on it
and that in the meanwhile
you get in-class time to work on your projects

BETH.
(raising her hand)
Miss Gallagher?

MISS GALLAGHER.
yes Beth

BETH.
sorry
we just kind of got
interrupted
when we were discussing the end of *The Crucible*?

and I feel like it would be really useful for our projects
to finish talking about it?

MISS GALLAGHER.
…
all right
would you like to lead a discussion?

BETH.
(SO excited but so flustered)
would I—?
um
yeah!
sure!
hold on lemme—
I have some notes

>*Beth scrambles in her bag for her notes*

MASON.
have you read *The Crucible*, Miss G?

MISS GALLAGHER.
I have
I read it when I was your age
in this very same classroom, actually

>*the students' minds are slightly blown by this*

BETH.
okay
um
I have my notes now

MISS GALLAGHER.
take it away, Miss Powell

BETH.
well I would love to get back to the whole thing we were um
debating

like
whether or not um
so Mr. Smith says that John Proctor is a hero
and that's clearly what Arthur Miller thought too
and all my research backs that up
every interpretation

IVY.
yeah the only person who didn't think so was Shelby

BETH.
yeah no I know
I think I just like
I don't know
okay so Mr. Smith always says to look at a character's first and last moments
and we already talked about when Proctor first comes in and it says
"on seeing him, Mary Warren leaps in fright"

NELL.
yeah but basically every stage direction about John Proctor is like
"storms in angrily with a deep rage" or something crazy

BETH.
totally
his anger absolutely has an arc throughout the
so okay um the ending
page one hundred and thirty-three[*] again

> *Beth picks up her script and flips to the end*
> *some people join her, some people ignore her*

right here where they're about to take John Proctor away
and he says to Elizabeth
um
Mason could you read it for us?

---

[*] or whatever page number it is in your edition

MASON.
(reading)
"Give them no tear! Tears pleasure them! Show honor now, show a stony heart and sink them with it!"

BETH.
great so yeah
that's John Proctor's last line
um
so do we think that supports or doesn't support the idea that John Proctor is a hero?

> *beat*

MASON.
I don't know if it really changes anything?
but like
I could be wrong

NELL.
yeah it seems like more of the same
like
"I have honor lalala"

BETH.
yeah
yeah I dunno I just wanted to revisit that moment in the light of okay so yeah moving on I really wanted to talk / about—

RAELYNN.
I actually feel like
um
…
sorry I

BETH.
no no go for it

RAELYNN.
um it's just like

John put Elizabeth through so much?
like SO much right?
and now like
he's about to *die*
and like pretty much as a direct result of what he did?
and he doesn't apologize?
and he tells her not to cry and not in a nice way?
and says nothing about like "hmmm let's take a second to figure out how you're gonna take care of yourself and our baby when I'm dead"

MISS GALLAGHER.
right!
he doesn't even tell her he loves her!
sorry to jump in
I just
I remember being your age and reading that part and feeling like
I don't know
my teacher said that John Proctor was this beacon of integrity
and it must be true, if a teacher said it, right?
but I guess I always kind of resented the idea that honor has to be
um
stony and stoic?
I guess?

BETH.
yeah wow that's like…
textbook toxic masculinity

RAELYNN.
exactly!
and he just um
I don't know
I mean he just tells her how to feel and how to act
and he's done it before in the play too
remember when he says he should have yelled at her instead of confessed to having an affair? how does he say it?

BETH.
(has this memorized)
"I should have roared you down when first you told me your suspicion. But I wilted, and like a Christian, I confessed."
act two

RAELYNN.
like…
yeah

MASON.
"roared you down"??
what a dick

NELL.
Rae, you're right

RAELYNN.
really?

NELL.
dude
yeah

BETH.
I never
I didn't even think about it like that
I'm sorry
I don't
I don't know why I didn't see it
now it seems so obvious
I'm so sorry
I shouldn't have been allowed to lead the discussion if I wasn't prepared

MISS GALLAGHER.
Beth, honey
you can stop apologizing
you don't have to apologize for existing

12.

> *later the same day*
> *after school*
> *Mason and Nell work on their project*
> *they're both studying their books*

MASON.
but the devil's not a character in the play

NELL.
or is he

MASON.
um
yeah
no
he's not
see?
character list
no devil

NELL.
he's a character in the minds of the townspeople
and the idea of him is visually represented by the yellow bird

MASON.
but are we even allowed to do something like that?
like with characters that aren't there?

NELL.
it's an interpretive assignment
we can do whatever we want

MASON.
yeah but like
well
okay
how do we do it?

NELL.
that's why we're meeting
that's the point of projects
we figure it out

MASON.
oh
okay
last project I got Beth and she basically just like
did all the work

NELL.
yeah that's Beth

MASON.
I feel like maybe it would have made me feel a little bad
but she seemed to really like doing it

NELL.
yeah
that's Beth
also I don't really believe you would've felt bad

MASON.
(his feelings are a little hurt)
…I feel bad about stuff

NELL.
if you say so

MASON.
I say so

NELL.
okay

> *beat*

Beth's such a trip
I think she just like
assumes I'm cool because I'm from somewhere else and she wants to *be* somewhere else?

but sometimes I worry everybody here's gonna like
find me out
'cause I'm super not cool
like
at all
I was actually kinda having a hard time before this
in Atlanta
with like
my friends
or "friends"
blehhh
this is boring, I'll stop

MASON.
I'm not bored
and you *are* cool

> *Nell makes a face*

I mean I think you are
I know you don't care what I think

NELL.
I don't Not care what you think
…
please don't tell anybody all that stuff
okay?

MASON.
I won't

> *a shared smile*
> *they return to their work*

wait
yellow birds are symbols for like the devil??
I totally missed that

NELL.
how are you in honors?

MASON.
I'm like really good at taking tests

NELL.
not all yellow birds are the devil
that's just what it means in *The Crucible*

MASON.
oh
okay
thanks
you're really smart

NELL.
I know

MASON.
damn
humble too

NELL.
I mean I'm not going to pretend I don't know something
if I already know it
that's part of what makes me smart

MASON.
hmm
yeah I guess that's a good point

NELL.
"we teach girls to shrink themselves
to make themselves smaller
we say
'you can have ambition
but not too much
otherwise you will threaten the man'"

MASON.
that sounds familiar

NELL.
it's in a Beyoncé song

MASON.
yes!!

NELL.
but it's actually from this talk by Chimamanda Ngozi Adichie

MASON.
we should use it as one of our outside source things!
I mean if you think it'd be good

NELL.
that could actually be really cool
I mean I don't know how it'll fit in

MASON.
yeah but
"that's the point of projects" right?
like you said?
we'll figure it out

Nell smiles

NELL.
yeah
we'll figure it out

beat

hey do you like
do you know Shelby very well?

MASON.
I mean
we've been in the same class since second grade
so I guess?
but also I don't really think I've ever had like
a real conversation with her
so I guess not

NELL.
yeah
I was just kinda wondering what you think about everything
since you've like
known her longer than I have

MASON.
yeah
yeah I don't know
I heard he just like
gave her a ride home one day and she tried something but he said no?
and I guess she got embarrassed?

NELL.
I mean I heard they had like a full-blown relationship

MASON.
dang
for real?

NELL.
yeah so who knows
I wish I could like reach out to her without it being weird
but I think it'd probably be weird
I don't know

>*beat*
>*Nell goes back to her book*
>*Mason smiles at Nell while she reads*

MASON.
hey Nell?
this might not be the best time to ask this or whatever but I'm just gonna go for it I mean um
do you wanna like
hang out?
like outside of class and feminist club?
I just
I'm really into how smart you are?

which is like a new thing for me and it really
I dunno
never mind
it's okay

>   *beat*

NELL.
yeah okay let's hang out

>   *Nell goes back to reading*

MASON.
yeah??

NELL.
do your work, Mason

MASON.
(immediately going back to his book)
on it

NELL.
just because you were sweet to me for like a second
doesn't mean I'm gonna do your work for you

MASON.
no no yeah for sure I don't want you to
this is fun

>   *he grins at her one last time, then goes back to reading*
>   *Nell watches him for a minute*
>   *she smiles*
>   *goes back to reading too*

13.

the next day, after school
Beth is alone in the classroom
she thinks she hears a noise outside and perks up
waits
nope
nothing
she gets up and starts to go to the door
just as she gets there, the door opens
it's Ivy
Beth screams
Ivy screams

IVY.
what the heck????

BETH.
you scared me!!!

IVY.
I'm sorry??

BETH.
I mean I didn't think anybody would actually come

IVY.
I mean yeah
I didn't really come for the club
this is just better than going home
and also I just
…
I miss you
I know that sounds stupid
I see you every day but you know / what I mean

BETH.
it doesn't sound stupid

IVY.
it's just been
I mean you know

BETH.
yeah

>   *beat*

IVY.
are we still best friends?

BETH.
of *course* we are

IVY.
okay

BETH.
we always have been and we *always* will be

IVY.
okay
cool
I just
I didn't know if you were mad at me or something

BETH.
what are you talking about?
why would I be mad at you?

IVY.
I didn't know if you were like
I know things with my dad have been
I know I haven't been like
my usual self

BETH.
well yeah I mean that's completely understandable, though

IVY.
yeah it's like

I mean
you know my dad's like weirdly my favorite person

BETH.
that's not weird

IVY.
I just
this is gonna sound so pathetic but
you and me haven't had a sleepover in like three weeks which is weird for us, you know?
and what if now you never wanna have a sleepover at my house again because you feel weird around my dad?
it's like
I dunno it's dumb I feel dumb
I don't even know / why I'm

>   *Beth interrupts Ivy by hugging her*
>   *they hug really tight*
>   *they love each other so much*
>   *mid hug, the door opens again*
>   *it's Raelynn and Nell*
>   *Beth is really excited to see them*

BETH.
you guys look Ivy's here!!
we're all here!

>   *she rushes to Raelynn and Nell and hugs them*

NELL.
okay calm down we saw you an hour ago

IVY.
she literally screamed when I came in
like a serial killer scream

NELL.
I don't know if serial killers are the screamers
right?
like I'm pretty sure their victims are the ones who scream

RAELYNN.
I wish we could scream or somethin

    beat

BETH.
my mom said the school board already met about Shelby
they're trying to like
be quiet about it

RAELYNN.
her parents wanted her to meet with my dad for like counseling but
he wanted to see what the school board decided first

IVY.
I heard she wasn't really staying with her aunt in Atlanta
she was at like a mental hospital

RAELYNN.
I mean
I don't think her family could like
afford that

BETH.
I know I'm supposed to believe women
like no matter what
but I just
I know him, you know?
he's like the best person I know
he's the *best* person
I just don't see how he
yeah

IVY.
I mean yeah
that's how I feel about my dad

    beat

BETH.
I hope he's okay

IVY.
yeah

BETH.
he's not returning my texts and I just
I hope he's okay

RAELYNN.
wait
you text him?

BETH.
yeah just sometimes
for like book recommendations or emergencies
and this is clearly an emergency

NELL.
…what other emergencies have there been?

BETH.
wait
are we even allowed to be meeting right now?
since he's not at school?

IVY.
I kinda feel like
nothing should happen to anybody until there's like
a trial
and then we can punish the men *if* they're proven guilty
but if we find out the girls are making it up
they should get punished just as bad

BETH.
that's like
I mean our justice system isn't really
like your dad can afford legal fees and good lawyers and stuff

RAELYNN.
also like
I think no matter what's true or like
not true

we have to remember that Shelby's clearly kind of going through something
and I mean like
we haven't really even listened to her yet

IVY.
it feels like
if you're accusing Mr. Smith of this
you're basically accusing my dad of the same thing

RAELYNN.
but like
your dad admitted that he did it

IVY.
my dad had a brief, consensual flirtation
it was a mistake
he's very ashamed
but he didn't just—
that lady is making it sound like it was all his fault
and I mean my dad didn't like
rape her
…
I know that's not the only bad thing that can happen
I just

    beat

NELL.
(to Beth)
I think it might be weird that you text Mr. Smith

BETH.
…
no
it's not
it's not like that
he's a really good teacher and he cares a lot and he's there for me
you and Ivy are the ones who talk about his like
his private parts

Ivy kinda half laughs
she can't help it

his PENIS
OKAY??
IS THAT BETTER
GOD
PENIS

then Beth screams
it feels so good
they all look at her
she stops
she's about to apologize, but then –
Raelynn screams
Beth and Raelynn scream together
Nell joins in
Ivy joins in
they scream so loud and for so long
it's a lifetime of screams
it's awesome
the classroom door opens
Mason and Lee come in
the girls stop screaming
beat

MASON.
what
the fuck

NELL.
we're stressed out

LEE.
are you guys doing actual witchcraft in here?

the classroom door opens
it's Shelby
oh shit
beat

SHELBY.
um
I need to
Rae? Beth?
can I talk to you two?

LEE.
isn't there a rule about like
extracurriculars if you don't come to class?
are you even allowed to be here?

SHELBY.
whatever
just
(to Raelynn and Beth)
please?

BETH.
I actually
um
I'm sorry but
I don't really know what to say to you right now

SHELBY.
I'm not asking you to say anything
I'm just asking you to listen

MASON.
I mean
(gesturing to Lee)
we already know you get around
if that's what you're gonna say

BETH.
Mason!

SHELBY.
okay so by your logic
I'm definitely telling the truth
wow, thank you so much for believing me, Mason!
thank you for being an ally

I feel a lot better now to know that even one shitty human being
who smells like cheese
is on my side

BETH.
he's not a shitty human being!

NELL.
yeah and he smells really good!

SHELBY.
just because he's your little pet project fucking feminist club mascot
and is actually performing like
basic human decency
sometimes instead of never
doesn't mean he's not shitty
y'all just have a really low bar for boys' behavior
which is like
I mean you guys you just
god
(to Beth)
you're a fuckin hypocrite

she leaves

NELL.
(to Mason)
why were you being a jerk

MASON.
I wasn't!!
geez!!
I was backing Beth up!

BETH.
I didn't say she got around

MASON.
yeah but you were all
you acted like you didn't

I mean you said we should support women!
I was supporting you!

NELL.
that's not what that means

RAELYNN.
I think I'm gonna
I need to
I'm gonna go check on her

LEE.
hey
Rae
wait a second
just
wait a second

RAELYNN.
what

LEE.
um
are you gonna come back?

RAELYNN.
I dunno

LEE.
okay I just thought like
we could maybe
Talk
after this

RAELYNN.
…

LEE.
I mean
I've been like
making a lot of effort

you know?
coming to these meetings?
I'm even being like
really vulnerable and stuff
saying this in front of people

    beat

RAELYNN.
so what
now you want like
a reward?

LEE.
no
I mean
no
I just wanna talk

RAELYNN.
what about

LEE.
a lot
things just like
we had that whole conversation
and then you / like never

RAELYNN.
oh that whole "conversation"?
do you mean like
when you threw a desk on the ground
and kiss-raped me?

LEE.
kiss-raped you??

RAELYNN.
I mean I guess the proper term would be like
sexual assault or harass/ment

LEE.
whoa whoa whoa whoa whoa whoa
okay
come on now

RAELYNN.
yeah
those are some of the terms we learn here
if you're so fucking interested in our fucking club

LEE.
whoa dude
you always yell at me for cussing

RAELYNN.
well sometimes, Lee
sometimes the only fucking word that fucking fits
what you're trying to fucking say is a fucking cuss word
so if you want to come to feminist club
because you *want* to then I will be happy to see you here
but I don't see the point in talking anymore
and to quote Taylor Swift
"we are never
ever
ever
ever
ever getting back together
like
ever"

    she leaves

14.

> *a little later, the same day*
> *outside a gas station*
> *Shelby and Raelynn are drinking slushies*

SHELBY.
so yeah
I didn't know how to tell you
but I also didn't know
how to *not* tell you?
it just
fuck
so yeah so I
I didn't like Plan it
with Lee
but I was obviously feeling like really messed up?
I mean I had been

> *she gestures around wildly, can't quite say "sleeping" or "having sex"*

with our *teacher*
for like *months*
which is *insane*
and I felt like
I dunno I think I felt really gross and weird and sad
and you know how sometimes you just need to like
dig yourself a deeper and deeper hole?
and like
boning Lee would make me feel grosser and weirder and sadder
I mean
I'm just gonna stop talking now

> *beat*
> *Raelynn laughs*

RAELYNN.
I can't believe you just said "boning"

in the middle of this like really serious conversation

> *Shelby starts laughing too*

SHELBY.
shut up

RAELYNN.
you're such an idiot

> *they both laugh*

I'm still
I'm still really mad at you

SHELBY.
okay

RAELYNN.
like about Lee a little
but it's not really that
I'm more just mad that you didn't talk to me
like you're my ride or die
how dare you

SHELBY.
do you believe me?

> *beat*

RAELYNN.
yeah
I do

> *Shelby nods*
> *pause*

I know the answer is probably "no"
but are you like
okay?

SHELBY.
yeah the answer is definitely no

but it's fine

    beat

RAELYNN.
you didn't like
I mean was there um
was there a particular reason you were gone for as long as you were?
like did you *need* to be gone for a certain amount of time?

SHELBY.
dude are you asking if I was pregnant?
is that what people think??

RAELYNN.
I don't think *all* people…

SHELBY.
fuck
I mean
no
I wasn't
I'm not
god
can you imagine?

    beat

RAELYNN.
are you staying in school?
are you allowed?

SHELBY.
I mean they're not gonna let me stay in his class
I don't remember the way they said it
but I'm a risk or something
a liability?
very cool thing to say to a literal child
anyway
whatever
he's coming back

it's like
official

RAELYNN.
god
are you serious?

SHELBY.
I mean I kinda saw it coming

    beat

RAELYNN.
what do you do for the rest of the year?

SHELBY.
supervised study hall aka sit in the library
then I have to finish lit this summer with a different teacher
but don't worry
we still get to finish our project
it'll be my grand finale
they wanna make sure like
your grade doesn't get messed with because of me

RAELYNN.
that's fucked up

SHELBY.
yeah

    beat

yeah

    beat

I wish we could do a project about the ocean
I've gotten really into the ocean
it's awesome
how little we know about it
and scary
I really like scary stuff lately

I dunno
it makes me feel better about my life to know that there are fish with teeth on the outside of their heads

RAELYNN.
totally

SHELBY.
I went to the aquarium a lot in Atlanta
my aunt has a pass

RAELYNN.
I wanna go!

SHELBY.
okay!

>   *beat*

but yeah
it's fine
he never teaches senior lit
so it's just this year

RAELYNN.
what do your parents think?

SHELBY.
they're like
you know with my um history of being a little crazy

RAELYNN.
you're not crazy

SHELBY.
I mean you know
you know how I get sometimes
you know how people like
I mean it's okay I'm fine but I'm
yeah
it's a Thing
and they're very Them about it

so obviously they think I'm me and Mr. Smith is just like
everything
because of church and stuff
they don't
I think they wanna make sure I can get through the year without burning it all down

>*beat*

RAELYNN.
what if we both did senior year in Atlanta
we could live with your aunt
I could get a weekend job and pay rent or like
I dunno
it's just for a year
then we can go anywhere

SHELBY.
yeah
maybe
…
also
I can't tell if we're There yet
but I'm just gonna gamble and say—
you kinda dodged a bullet with Lee in terms of the
he is like
Not good at doing his job
and I am amazing at doing mine?
felt very unfair

>*Raelynn laughs and is scandalized at herself for laughing*

RAELYNN.
well he hadn't really done it before!
cut him some slack!

SHELBY.
I mean sure
but there are ways to learn like
while you're in the thick of it

RAELYNN.
oh my god

>*they laugh*

SHELBY.
you can also just ask?
do boys not get that?

RAELYNN.
do boys get anything?

>*they laugh some more*
>*beat*

SHELBY.
that's the thing, though
with Carter—
Mr.—
yeah
he like
he asked a lot of stuff
not even sex stuff
like
stuff about my life
stuff about me
I mean he
yeah
I really liked that

>*beat*
>*Shelby shakes her head really fast*

say something dumb
distract me

RAELYNN.
ummmm
I mean was it good enough to wear the Town Slut badge with honor?
(valley girl voice)
because it's so pretty on you

they both burst out laughing

SHELBY.
are we even allowed to be laughing?

RAELYNN.
I think that's up to you

SHELBY.
judging by everything I know
I mean
I think I'm probably gonna be super messed up for a really long time?
but I don't know if I'm like
fully equipped to start that journey right now
I think that'll kinda just come whenever it comes
so yeah
I dunno
I think we're allowed to laugh

Raelynn laughs a very exaggerated and insane laugh
Shelby does her own version
they trade crazy laughs back and forth
somewhere along the way, crazy laughing turns into real laughing
oh no now they can't <u>stop</u> laughing
they laugh and they laugh
it's the kind of laughing that goes on for so long it stops being funny
then it's funny again
their stomachs hurt from it
they laugh for way, way longer than you think they should
they might hold hands, or lean heads against shoulders
the audience should absolutely get a little uncomfortable from how long they laugh
if you think they're laughing long enough, they almost definitely probably aren't
the laughter might turn a little manic in an edge-of-tears way but still
they laugh

15.

> *the next week*
> *lunchtime*

MR. SMITH.
thanks for coming in early

BETH.
of course

> *beat*

MR. SMITH.
I know those lunchtime minutes are precious

BETH.
no no
I'm
of course

> *beat*

MR. SMITH.
how have you been?

BETH.
…I've been okay
it's been
I've been okay

> *beat*

it's kind of surreal
to see you back
it feels like it's been forever

MR. SMITH.
I know
I can't believe it
I mean I'm

Miss Gallagher's gonna be sitting in on classes for the rest of the year

BETH.
she was actually
it was great to have her
she had some good stuff to say

MR. SMITH.
that's awesome

BETH.
I mean obviously we missed you a ton

MR. SMITH.
well thanks
that's sweet of you

    beat

BETH.
I haven't really heard much news about the details of

MR. SMITH.
you know
without saying too much
there just wasn't a lot of proof
and the school board called into question the character
of uh

    beat

BETH.
that's great

    beat

MR. SMITH.
gosh Beth
I'm just
I've been totally sick over this

    beat

I need to know
I
no
I'm sorry
that's inappropriate

BETH.
what?

MR. SMITH.
I wanted to know if
if you believed me
but that's
I can't ask you that

BETH.
oh

> *beat*

MR. SMITH.
I just don't know what I'm going to do
you know?

BETH.
I think
maybe
it'll blow over?

MR. SMITH.
I don't want you to feel like I'm putting you in a bad position

BETH.
no
I don't feel that way

MR. SMITH.
it's just that you're one of the only friends I've got left
I mean
that's probably the last thing I should say now
but I really miss our talks

BETH.
I do too

> *beat*

MR. SMITH.
my wife doesn't believe me
she says she does
but

BETH.
I'm
sure she'll come around
you two have such a special—
I'm so sorry

> *beat*

MR. SMITH.
it really felt like
for a while
that my life was over
…
it got to the point where I was thinking
"this is it. I'm just going to kill myself. they'd all be better off without / me"

BETH.
no no no no don't say that please don't say that
…
I wouldn't be better off

> *beat*
> *Mr. Smith smiles at her*

MR. SMITH.
it feels really good to be back
to see you
what have you been reading lately?

16.

later the same day, right before class
it's day one of class project presentations
before the bell
Miss Gallagher and Mr. Smith meet

MISS GALLAGHER.
so I just wanted to make sure we both understand why I'll be here
the school board felt like it would be a good way to cover our bases
and after today I'll really just be a
presence
I'll monitor and provide accounts to the administration and be here for the students if they have any questions or concerns but
I won't say anything during class unless I need to
and I won't interfere with your authority
today, though, it's a little tricky
since Shelby will be here for one day only, it would be great if I could kind of take the lead this time
and have you just solely be taking notes for grading purposes

MR. SMITH.
whatever you think is best

MISS GALLAGHER.
great
well then unless you have any / questions—

MR. SMITH.
I just wish I had seen this coming
you know?
I mean
I saw that she had a crush on me
I knew there's been a history of
how did you say it?
concerning behavior?
anyway, I knew that and I didn't shut it down
that's on me
I just had no idea she would—

it's crazy
I like to think the best of people
especially my students

MISS GALLAGHER.
right

MR. SMITH.
anyway
it's all taken care of now
and thank you for being here
I'm really lucky to have you, Bailey
(checks watch)
almost time to get started!

MISS GALLAGHER.
…
you know
I'm a tri delt

MR. SMITH.
nice
I'm delta tau delta

MISS GALLAGHER.
my grand-big was Lorin Kerr
do you know her?
she's from Russell County?

MR. SMITH.
Lorin Kerr…

MISS GALLAGHER.
she was a senior in high school when you were a senior in college
she met you at a party

MR. SMITH.
what a small world
you know, it's been so long
I'm terrible with names

MISS GALLAGHER.
yeah
it's funny, though
she remembered you real well
her little did too

>*beat*

and I knew Ellen
I mean just a little
through Fran
but I heard about all your
yeah

MR. SMITH.
Ellen and I had a very
complicated relationship
and it was a long time ago

MISS GALLAGHER.
I didn't believe them
any of them
because you were you
because I knew you
my brother knew you
everybody knew you
you were always so nice to me
…
so there must have been a misunderstanding, right?
they must have just gotten confused?
they were all crazy?

>*the bell rings*
>*students start shuffling in*

welcome, welcome everybody!
as soon as we've taken our seats we'll just dive right in

>*Shelby and Raelynn come in wearing full-out 1600s attire*
>*or like, at least their non-budget version of full-out*
>*definitely at least bonnets*

*one of them carries a visible music-playing device: speaker,
boom box, phone, etc.
they're nervous*

oh my goodness, you two look amazing!
why don't you go ahead and get set up right here at the front

*they stand at the front of the classroom
get their music all ready to go, check in with each other*

all right
everybody settle down
whenever you're ready, ladies

SHELBY.
um
we'd like to start with an outside reading?

RAELYNN.
from sparknotes

*they stare at Mr. Smith and the rest of the class for a second
they dare them to question the validity of sparknotes*

"Honest, upright, and blunt-spoken, John Proctor is a good man, but one with a secret, fatal flaw."

SHELBY.
"Proctor is, above all, a proud man who places great emphasis on his reputation."

RAELYNN.
"He finally bursts out with a confession, calling Abigail a 'whore.'"

SHELBY.
"He goes to the gallows redeemed for his earlier sins."

RAELYNN.
a good man

SHELBY.
a proud man

RAELYNN.
whore

SHELBY.
(making excuses)
but he's such a good man

RAELYNN.
(making excuses)
he's a very proud man

SHELBY.
think about his reputation

RAELYNN.
whore

> *they sharp-turn to face each other*

RAELYNN.
(as Elizabeth)
hello, Abigail Williams

SHELBY.
(as Abigail)
hello, Elizabeth Proctor
…
well
now that we've got the stiff pleasantries out of the way

RAELYNN.
(as Elizabeth)
yes
now that the audience knows who we are
we can begin

SHELBY.
(as Abigail)
do I start?

RAELYNN.
(as Elizabeth)
you know
I'm not sure
we don't really talk to each other in this play

SHELBY.
(as Abigail)
do you at least know what we're supposed to talk *about*?

RAELYNN.
(as Elizabeth)
I assume John

SHELBY.
(as Abigail)
that seems like a good assumption
I assume I'm also supposed to apologize at some point

RAELYNN.
(as Elizabeth)
yes that's probably expected

> *up until this point, there may have been a ~performance~ to the way they're playing Abigail and Elizabeth all of that should fall away now*

SHELBY.
(as Abigail)
I don't really *want* to apologize, though?

RAELYNN.
(as Elizabeth)
that's okay
I don't really want to talk about John

SHELBY.
(as Abigail)
oh good
I'm just kind of

RAELYNN.
(as Elizabeth)
sick of him?

SHELBY.
(as Abigail)
exactly!!

RAELYNN.
(as Elizabeth)
can I ask you a question?

SHELBY.
(as Abigail)
sure

RAELYNN.
(as Elizabeth)
why did you dance

SHELBY.
(as Abigail)
in the woods?

RAELYNN.
(as Elizabeth)
were there other times not in the woods?

SHELBY.
(as Abigail)
oh yeah
I dance all the time
it's really fun

RAELYNN.
(as Elizabeth)
but it's not allowed

SHELBY.
(as Abigail)
but why not

RAELYNN.
(as Elizabeth)
because of god

SHELBY.
(as Abigail)
I don't know
I think god would like it
they say he wouldn't but
part of what I learned from all this
is that all these men in charge?
they just make stuff up
they just make up whatever suits them
whenever it suits them

RAELYNN.
(as Elizabeth)
they say it's because they know best

SHELBY.
(as Abigail)
well if they say it, it must be true

RAELYNN.
(as Elizabeth)
they were scared of you
you made them scared

SHELBY.
(as Abigail)
being scary was even more fun than dancing
they actually paid attention when I was scary

RAELYNN.
(as Elizabeth)
but you were lying
weren't you?

SHELBY.
(as Abigail)
I told the truth about John Proctor

he didn't like that very much
no one listened when I told the truth

RAELYNN.
(as Elizabeth)
I don't know if I've ever been scary
I don't know if I know how
maybe things would be different if I did

SHELBY.
(as Abigail)
yeah but
it shouldn't take being scary to make things different
they shouldn't have to be scared into listening to us
things should just *be different*
they should just *listen*

> *the following unfolds the way fire does:*
> *a spark, then a flame, then a roar, then a sustained burn*

RAELYNN.
(as Elizabeth)
one day
maybe
the new world we were promised
will actually be new
one day
maybe
the men in charge
won't be in charge anymore
one day we can dance in the forest
and in the streets
and with each other
in our rooms that belong to us and only to us
on our beds we share with no one
under the moon
under the sun
under the shade of our favorite trees

under a shower of the blood and brittle bones of supposedly strong men who failed us
and when that day comes
it won't matter that we're not supposed to dance
it won't matter that once upon a time
I married a man who made me feel smaller than nothing
and like his shame was my shortcoming
it won't matter that when you were sixteen and newly orphaned
a married man two decades older than you made promises he had no intention to keep
and said things in the dark that made you feel like you were made of fire
it *will* matter that you took that fire and burned him down with it because that same fire will spread
it will scorch the earth to make room for the new world we deserve
it won't matter that he told you and told me it was all our fault
each of us
both of us
it won't matter that we let him think he had reclaimed his goodness in the face of death
it won't matter because that kind of currency has been out-of-date for centuries in our new world
those feelings will be so far away from us by then
at first we won't remember their names
and that will plague us
then the faces of those feelings will become blurry
and we'll feel the stirrings of peace
and then we won't remember those feelings at all
we wouldn't even recognize them if they passed us on the street
we'll sleep soundly then
we'll use our fire only for warmth

> *Shelby presses play on the music, maybe after they check in with each other first*
> *Lorde's "Green Light"* starts to play*
> *god that song is so good*

---

* see special note on songs/recordings on the copyright page.

and just fyi this sequence needs <u>the whole song</u> to get to where it needs to go
I promise
during the first verse, they perform a series of precise, synchronized movements
it might be hard for Shelby to fully commit for the first part of the dance
she might even have to stop once or twice –
I mean, Mr. Smith is Right There
but she's so fucking brave and she keeps going
because Raelynn's Right There too
they're doing this together
that's all Shelby needs
then during the pre-chorus key change, when it's like "but I hear sounds in my mind"
Shelby and Raelynn start to nod their heads and really feel the beat
it escalates – nodding spreads to shoulders to feet to whole bodies
by the time the chorus hits, they are dancing full-out
wild and free, big and chaotic
hair flying, limbs flailing – but still choreographed
the second verse comes
they keep dancing, a return to a more contained choreography
they travel all over the classroom
when the second verse is halfway over and it's clear they aren't gonna stop dancing:

MR. SMITH.
(shouting over the music)
all right, that's your time
five minutes is up
thank you very much, ladies

> *they keep dancing*
> *the music gets louder*

ladies

they keep dancing
Mr. Smith stands up and starts to approach the dancing to stop it
all of a sudden, Nell stands up too
she starts dancing
the class looks at her like "is this part of the project?"
she dances into Mr. Smith's path
like "no way are you gonna stop them if I have anything to say about it"
she goes to dance with Shelby and Raelynn
they welcome her
the music gets louder

all right, ladies

Mason stands up
this moment's not about him
he knows it's not
but he really wants to show his support
he does a sweet little dance at his desk

Mr. Smith starts to walk closer to stop the dancing
he barely takes a step, though –
Miss Gallagher stands up
gives him a Look
he stops

others might get up and dance too, if you have others
but it should never end up being more than half the class dancing
otherwise it's too easy

somewhere along the way –
toward the end of the dance but not so much that there's no time –
it starts to look less like a dance and more like an exorcism

maybe we see the moon
maybe we see fire
maybe not

then, when the song starts to go into that slower moment at the end:
Beth stands up
she looks a little surprised at herself
the other girls see her
we see them see her
she takes a step toward them
is she going to dance too?
she might
she just might

blackout

end of play

Hello, actors, theatre makers, and theatre fans,

On behalf of Broadway Licensing Global and the author(s) of this work, we thank you for your continued support of the arts and the playwrights you love.

Like every title in our catalogue, this play is covered by copyright law, which ensures authors are rewarded for creating new dramatic work and protects them from theft and abuse of their work. We are compelled to impress upon all who obtain this edition that **this text may not be copied, distributed, or publicly produced in any way**, nor uploaded to any file-sharing websites or software—public or private. Any such action has an immediate and negative effect on the livelihood of the writer(s)—it is also stealing and is against the law. As a result, should you copy, distribute, or publicly produce any part of this text without express written consent and licensed permission from our company—even if no one is being paid and/or admission is not being charged—your organization shall be subject to legal consequences that we are sure you want to avoid.

But we have faith in you and your understanding of these guidelines!

While this acting edition is the only approved text for performance, there may be other editions of the play available for sale. It is important to note that our team has worked with the playwright(s) to ensure this published acting edition reflects their desired text for all future productions. If you have purchased a revised edition from us, that is the only edition you may use for performance, unless explicitly stated in writing by our team.

Finally, and this is an important one, **this script cannot be changed in any way** without written permission from our team. That said, feel free to reach out to us. We don't bite, and we are always happy to have a discussion to see if we can accommodate your request.

We are thrilled this play has made it into your hands and we hope you love it as much as we do. Thank you for helping us keep the theatre alive and well, and for supporting playwrights, in our continued journey to make everyone a theatre person!

Sincerely,
Fellow theatre lovers at Broadway Licensing Global

Note on Songs/Recordings, Images, or Other Production Design Elements

Be advised that Broadway Licensing neither holds the rights to nor grants permission to use any songs, recordings, images, or other design elements mentioned in the play. It is the responsibility of the producing theater/organization to obtain permission of the copyright owner(s) for any such use. Additional royalty fees may apply for the right to use copyrighted materials.

For any songs/recordings, images, or other design elements mentioned in the play, works in the public domain may be substituted. It is the producing theater/organization's responsibility to ensure the substituted work is indeed in the public domain. Broadway Licensing cannot advise as to whether or not a song/arrangement/recording, image, or other design element is in the public domain.